MW00562742

Sensory Motor Handbook

A Guide for Implementing and Modifying Activities in the Classroom

Julie Bissell, M.A., OTR

Jean Fisher, M.A., OTR

Carol Owens, OTR

Patricia Polcyn, OTR

HAMMILL INSTITUTE ON DISABILITIES
8700 SHOAL CREEK BOULEVARD
AUSTIN, TEXAS 78757-6897
512/451-3521 FAX 512/451-3728

SII
Sensory Integration International

© 1988, 1998 by Sensory Integration International

Published by

H Hammill Institute on Disabilities
8700 Shoal Creek Boulevard
Austin, Texas 78757-6897
512/451-3521 Fax 512/451-3728

Gertie Ball is a registered trademark of Small World Toys.
Lego is a registered trademark of Lego Systems, Inc.
Nerf is a registered trademark of Hasbro, Inc.
Tinkertoy is a registered trademark of Playschool, Inc., a subsidiary of Hasbro, Inc.
Wiffle Ball is a registered trademark of The Wiffle Ball, Inc.

The Library of Congress has this Catalog-in-Publication information:
Sensory motor handbook: a guide for implementing and modifying
     activities in the classroom / Julie Bissell . . . [et al.].—2nd. ed.
          p. cm.
     Includes bibliographical references and index.
        ISBN 0-7616-4386-9
     1. Activity programs in education—Handbooks, manuals, etc. 2. Perceptual-motor learning—
Handbooks, manuals, etc. 3. Teaching—Aids and devices—Handbooks, manuals, etc. I. Bissell, Julie.
LB1027.25.S46   1998
371.91'6—dc21   98-16011
                                                                                                        CIP

Currently Hammill Institute on Disabilities
ISBN-13: 978-160251012-8
ISBN-10: 160251012-1

Previously published by PsychCorp, a division of Harcourt Assessment, Inc.,
under ISBN 0761643869.

Printed in the United States of America

2 3 4 5 6 7   14 13 12 11 10 09

To A. Jean Ayres, who dedicated her life to understanding and helping children with special needs.

Acknowledgments

The authors would like to acknowledge the special education staff of the Anaheim City School District SELPA and the Greater Anaheim SELPA. It is the sincerity and team spirit alive in these districts that enables us all to help children be the best that they can be. We appreciate the creative feedback that we have received over the years as we field tested, modified, and reworked many of our activities in the classroom.

A special thank you is in order for William A. Thompson and Ann Beavers, who initially inspired us to take our work from the clinic and perfect it in the classroom so that more teachers and children could benefit from our knowledge. We would like to recognize the work of Stephanie Pollard, MA, CCC, SP, Ann Stone, MA, CCC, SP, and Erin Garcia, CCC, SP, for their expertise in the revision of this book.

Sensory Integration International, Stephen Leinau, Zoe Mailloux, MA, OTR, FAOTA, Irene Bagge, and the Stairwell Group assisted in the organization of the original publication. Debora Skarsaug Crowley, OTR/L, Mary Jane Zehnpfennig, MA, OTR, Babetta Velategui, OTR, and Carol Hamilton Dodd, MA, OTR, will always be remembered for their ideas in the initiation of this project.

About the Authors

Julie Bissell, M.A., OTR, graduated from the University of California, Santa Barbara with a bachelor of arts degree in ergonomics and physical education. She completed a master of arts degree in occupational therapy through the University of Southern California. She worked with A. Jean Ayres, Ph.D., OTR, FAOTA, and helped to collect normative data for the Sensory Integration and Praxis Tests (SIPT). She is certified to administer and interpret the SIPT. She has coordinated occupational therapy and physical therapy services for the Anaheim City School District for the past 16 years, developing programs for children with specific learning disabilities, autism, developmental delays, multiple handicaps, orthopedic handicaps, attention deficit, sensory processing disorders, and emotional disturbance. Julie serves on the Board of Counselors for the USC Department of Occupational Science and Occupational Therapy.

Jean Fisher, M.A., OTR, graduated from Mount St. Mary's College with a degree in art and a minor in chemistry. She received a certificate and a master of arts degree in occupational therapy from the University of Southern California. She has been practicing occupational therapy for 37 years. She set up an Occupational Therapy Department at the University of California, Los Angeles Medical Center in the early 1960s and worked as an independent contractor and feeding consultant with cerebral palsy children in the 1970s. She has worked with individuals of all ages, focusing on children from preschool to sixth grade. Jean works as a consultant for five Orange County school districts, including the Anaheim City School District. She designs and implements activities for more than 25 classrooms, serving students who have hearing losses, multiple and orthopedic handicaps, developmental or learning disabilities, autism, and severe, emotional disorders.

Carol Owens, OTR, graduated from San Jose State University with a bachelor of science degree in occupational therapy. She has worked for the past 20 years in the California public school system, including 16 years with the Anaheim City School District, serving students who have neurodevelopmental delays and orthopedic handicaps. Carol has developed extensive occupational therapy programs for children who have visual handicaps and autism. She is certified to administer and interpret the SIPT. Her practice includes children with specific learning disabilities, autism, visual handicaps, sensory processing problems, and attention deficit disorders.

Patricia Polcyn, OTR, graduated from Western Michigan University with a bachelor of science degree in occupational therapy in 1977. She began her career in occupational therapy in private practice, working in mental health settings, using a sensory integration frame of reference. She is certified to administer and interpret SIPT. Patricia is self-employed, and her practice involves provision of occupational therapy services for six public school districts in Orange County, California. Patricia works with students who have severe handicaps, multiple handicaps, specific learning disabilities, autism, sensory processing disorders, attention deficits, and a variety of other diagnoses. She lectures for local colleges, parent groups, and school district staff. She is a fieldwork supervisor for OT and COTA students and has contracts with a number of colleges and universities.

Contents

Preface

Occupational therapists, teachers, and parents are constantly searching for resources to help children who experience difficulties in the classroom and in everyday play. We are occupational therapists with extensive experience in education and knowledge of the neurological principles underlying the development of sensory processing and motor performances as they relate to learning and behavior. This manual was written, purposely avoiding medical terminology, to assist both the professional and layperson working with children in special education.

Problems in the development of attention, direction-following, creative imagination, eye-hand coordination, self-esteem, and social appropriateness often are observed in children with special needs and sometimes can be related to faulty perception of sensory information. When faced with developmental delays, sensory processing problems, or poor motor coordination, therapists, teachers, and parents need to identify activities that really work to meet the varied needs of these children.

The activities have proved successful in a variety of situations, ranging from regular education classrooms to those serving children with multiple handicaps. The activities are easy to implement, require a minimal amount of equipment, and will create enjoyable and memorable childhood experiences. Many traditional children's games, songs, and rhymes are presented in original and modified versions. This enables challenged students to be a part of the heritage and rich tradition of American play.

This book provides teachers with a framework from which to observe, modify, and implement motor-related activities in the classroom. Occupational therapists can use it as a springboard for the many classroom activity analyses that only they can provide. It was created for this purpose with great care.

Introduction

When a teacher asks, "What can I do to meet sensory and motor needs in my classroom?" or when a parent asks "What can I do at home?", the *Sensory Motor Handbook* will provide hundreds of answers. In this book you will find activities that meet individual, small group, and classroom needs. It is written for the entire education team, ranging from occupational therapists, physical therapists, speech therapists, school psychologists, and teachers to parents, grandparents and babysitters. This book can be used to access activities directly or as a resource for educational professionals planning and providing consultation services.

The purpose of this book is to provide the educational team with an understanding of the relevance of sensory and motor factors to learning and behavior. It is a tool to empower educators and parents with plans of action to help children develop the sensory and motor foundations needed to function in the classroom.

Important sensory and motor systems are defined and described in terms of normal development and classroom behavior. The *Troubleshooting* section is a valuable tool for assisting with classroom modifications for individual children. Ten common classroom situations are analyzed, and many suggestions are presented in this chapter.

Traditional children's games, chants, and activities are used and modified for all levels of participation. These games have been designed and modified to maximize the amount of sensory and motor benefit to the children as they learn to organize their behavior in play situations. A chart at the beginning of each chapter identifies the value of each activity by indicating the primary sensory and motor areas that are challenged. Each activity includes teacher observation tips. To better meet the needs of the education team working in the classroom, the activities are organized according to equipment. This makes it easier to plan and prepare for classroom activities. There are ball and balloon games, beanbag games, games with easily made equipment, traditional children's games, oral motor activities, and tool activities.

The activities and classroom modifications are appropriate for children from age three and adults of all ages ranging from those in regular education classrooms to those with multiple handicaps. Each activity page offers suggestions for variations and modifications.

The *Troubleshooting* section further breaks down strategies for organizing behavior during motor time, improving sportsmanship and cooperation, and working with a broad range of skills in the same classroom. While there are not always easy solutions to classroom problems, many modifications are presented that can be considered, attempted, and implemented.

Many teachers have reported that in using these activities and modifications, students are observed to experience less stress in the classroom. Because many basic sensory and motor needs are addressed, students more easily learn to adapt to and master a variety of sensory, motor, and behavior challenges during the school day. As sensory and motor needs are met, children begin to experience a degree of success that enables them to be more confident and effective as students.

Auditory Processing

Auditory processing is the ability to perceive and understand what is heard in the environment. This involves more than the sense of hearing. Understanding auditory information requires intricate processing. Discriminating, associating, and interpreting sounds; remembering and comprehending what is heard; and relating words in a meaningful way are all parts of auditory processing.

Auditory processing plays an important role in children's classroom performance. Children who experience difficulty processing what they hear may at times appear confused or inattentive. They may haphazardly rush into tasks and may take a long time to respond to directions and to complete tasks. They may overrespond to competing noise in the environment. Remembering and sequencing multiple-step directions may require added concentration and effort. Good auditory processing is an important foundation for development of language skills. It is critical in the communication and comprehension of action plans. It can have an impact on peer relationships and productivity in the classroom. Children who have difficulty understanding the spoken word often depend upon the visual system to gain information.

Auditory processing is nurtured and challenged when children listen to and are involved in conversations, stories, rhymes, songs, and music. Speaking slowly and clearly while reducing complex conversations to simple concrete statements helps facilitate the development of auditory processing.

Body Awareness

Awareness of the body comes from sensations from muscles and joints. The term "proprioception" is often used to refer to this sensory system. Receptors located in the muscles and joints tell the brain when and how the muscles are contracting or stretching and when and how the joints are bending, extending, or being pulled and compressed. This information enables a person to know without looking where each part of the body is and how it is moving through space.

The muscles, joints, and brain provide each other with vital sensory information to make spatial and temporal adjustments in movement possible. Integration of this information enables children to execute gross and fine motor activities that require subtle variations in posture, strength, force, and dexterity. Children with poor awareness of body parts tend to rely on visual information and may not be able to move properly if they cannot see where their arms and legs are. Without this visual information, they may fall out of their seats. They may have only vague awareness of their position in space and have a difficult time getting dressed or into and out of a car.

Children with poor body awareness may have difficulty knowing where their bodies are in relation to objects. They frequently break toys because they do not know how much pressure they are exerting when putting things together or pulling things apart. They may have poor fine motor control because they cannot accurately feel where or how their arms, forearms, hands, or fingers are moving and do not have precise information about the tools in their hands. They typically press too hard or too softly with pencils. Children with problems in this area may appear sloppy or clumsy, or have disorganized personal belongings.

Information regarding body awareness is provided to the brain when muscles and joints are working against gravity or resistance. This occurs normally in development when children crawl, climb, lift, swim, walk up hills, carry heavy objects, and push and pull objects, such as push toys and wagons, against resistance. These types of play activities can improve body awareness by giving additional information to the muscles, joints, and brain through resistance and heavy work.

Coordination of Body Sides

The ability to coordinate the right and left sides of the body and to cross the midline of the body is an indication that both sides of the brain are working well together and sharing information efficiently. Coordination of the two body sides is an important foundation for the development of many gross and fine motor skills. It is essential to the development of cerebral specialization for skilled use of a dominant hand.

Children with poor coordination of the two body sides may adjust their bodies to avoid crossing the midline. They may not be able to coordinate one hand to move while the other hand is acting as an assist to stabilize the project. They may switch hands during a fine motor task because they are experiencing frustration with using the two hands together.

Good coordination of the two body sides is an important foundation for writing with pencils and cutting with scissors. The ability to coordinate the two body sides is first observed when babies transfer objects from one hand to another, bang two blocks together, bring their hands to their mouths, or imitate pat-a-cake. Children begin to coordinate their body sides when they manipulate toys such as pop beads and blocks, and learn to skip, gallop, play rhythm games, turn a jump rope, or ride a bike. Many traditional children's games and activities offer good opportunities to improve the coordination of the two body sides. Hand clapping to songs and rhymes, tossing and catching objects, and tapping rhythm sticks are favorites.

Fine Motor

Fine motor control is the ability to use one's hands and fingers precisely in a skilled activity. Good fine motor skill stems from solid sensory and motor foundations. For good fine motor control, it is important to have muscle and joint stability, especially in the neck, trunk, and upper extremities. One's eye muscles must work in a coordinated manner to quickly localize and track objects in the environment and smoothly guide the hand. Subconscious awareness of where and how hands and fingers are moving in space, accurate tactile discrimination, and hand strength aid in the control of objects of various sizes, weights, shapes, and textures. The ability to judge the visual spatial relationship of objects accurately is essential for the precision required in fine motor control. The ability to motor plan, (that is, to organize and carry out a sequence of unfamiliar motor tasks) is involved in many fine motor activities. Coordination of the two sides of the body is essential to fine motor coordination and the development of hand dominance.

Hand use developmentally precedes tool use. Through a progression of hand movements, a child gradually acquires the precision needed for fine motor skill with tools. Following is a brief overview of the significance and development of hand control.

Gross Grasp

The progression of early grasp patterns begins with the use of the whole hand from a raking approach to a palmar grasp that uses the fingers to press the object against the palm. The thumb then becomes incorporated into the grasp pattern.

The whole hand is used to hang on to the object without isolating the use of various fingers. Strength of grasp becomes a critical factor as the infant becomes mobile. A secure grasp is part of the foundation for pulling up to the standing position. It enables the child to secure objects for climbing, pushing, and pulling. Gross grasp is challenged when a child hangs on to ropes when swinging, hangs from monkey bars, or plays tug-of-war.

Gross Release

Developmentally, the ability to grasp and hold an object is followed by a gross release. Initially, release is crude and somewhat random. Refining the ability to release gives the child greater control over objects. Children practice and refine their ability to release through play as they grasp and let go of toys. Opportunities in play to stack blocks, put things in containers, and toss beanbags or balls help refine these skills.

Fine Grasp

Fine grasp is characterized by the ability to control each finger independently and in relation to the thumb. This ability develops as children learn to point their index fingers, poke at objects, and pick up small objects. The children then incorporate the middle finger into their pinch patterns, which provides a more secure fine grasp pattern. The ring and little finger move into the palm to provide stability so that the thumb, index, and middle finger can work together. Skill and dexterity in using fine grasp is challenged as the children finger feed and play with pegs, beads, and crayons. Prewriting skills emerge.

Timed Grasp and Release

Once a child has practiced grasp and release in a random fashion, an element of timing emerges. Timing refers to choosing an appointed or fixed moment for something to happen, begin, or end. Timing a motor response is a critical component of hand dexterity. Timing is developed for gross motor activities when a child motor plans the actions of his whole body. In fine motor activities, timing for precision is practiced when a child uses eating utensils, throws and catches beanbags and balls, and begins to use a variety of tools.

Hand Dominance

Many children who have fine motor problems may not have established hand dominance. Genetics, sensory processing, and overall motor coordination can affect the development of hand dominance.

Children are thought to be genetically predisposed toward developing a preference for one hand over the other for fine motor precision. Inefficient central nervous system processing can interfere with the genetic urge to use a dominant hand. It has been hypothesized (Ayres, 1979; DiQuiros and Schrager, 1978) that when a brain is struggling with inefficient or faulty interpretation of sensory information, the development of hand dominance is compromised.

Overall motor coordination is an important foundation for the development of hand dominance. Hand dominance can be thought of as an end product of earlier developmental steps. The development of good coordination between the two body sides and the ability to plan, time, and sequence an activity gives a child confidence to rely on one hand for tasks requiring precision.

Children who have the opportunity to develop solid sensory and motor foundations may automatically establish hand dominance. If however, by the age of 6, they have not established hand dominance, they should be encouraged to concentrate on using a dominant hand. Through observation, testing, and a review of family handedness, a recommendation of which hand to encourage can be made. Children can then better organize consistent strategies for fine motor work.

Tool Control

Before children can use tools in a coordinated manner, they must have basic control over their hands. The development of a gross grasp is important to overall strength and stability when holding a tool. Fine grasp is necessary to allow each finger and the thumb to accommodate a wide variety of tools. The overall ability to coordinate the body sides is essential to provide stability with one hand while the other hand is engaged in a task requiring precision in movement. Timing of grasp and release and motor planning ability are important to execute quick and accurate control over tools.

Motor Planning

Motor planning, or praxis, is the ability to conceive of an idea and to organize and carry out a sequence of unfamiliar actions. Motor planning is the first step in learning new skills. Good motor planning ability requires accurate information from all sensory systems of the body.

Sensations from the eyes, ears, skin, muscle, joints, and the vestibular system provide the brain with basic and essential information. This information is necessary in order to organize sensory impulses to plan, organize, time, and sequence an unfamiliar task. If a basic sensory component is contributing faulty information or operating slowly, motor planning ability could be seriously compromised.

Children with poor motor planning may seem clumsy, accident prone, and messy. They may experience a prolonged period of struggle in attempting to master a new skill and therefore establish routines to eliminate the need for unfamiliar movement. They may be able to compensate for a lack of accurate sensory information by figuring out the demands of a task cognitively, but may expend undue mental energy in doing so. They may spend time attending to other children's activity, and may be verbally manipulative in order to avoid having to perform. Children may imitate the actions of other children rather than try to initiate the activity themselves. Some children may even experience difficulty imitating the actions of others and find it difficult to follow the teacher's visual instructions.

Motor planning abilities are challenged in the classroom each time a child is presented with a variation of a familiar motor task or with a new assignment. When learning to write or cut with scissors, a child synthesizes a variety of sensory information to plan and sequence each stroke or cut in order to successfully complete the task. A child with a motor planning problem may have significant difficulty finishing work on time because he or she does not know how to start or finish the task. Another child may rush through the task without being able to recognize the parts or steps of the task as they relate to the end product. This child typically turns in messy, haphazard work.

Children develop the ability to motor plan as they interact with their environment and are required to make an adaptive response to an unfamiliar activity. Through play, children explore the use of many objects and develop creative ideas. Motor planning develops when children experiment with how their bodies relate to space and how parts relate to a whole in such toys as puzzles and simple take-apart toys or models. Children learn to imitate when playing pat-a-cake, peek-a-boo, and later games such as *Simon Says, Mother May I,* and *Follow the Leader.* Motor planning is further developed when children are asked to sequence several motor actions in a new skill or to follow several directions in an unfamiliar task.

Ocular Control

Ocular control is the smooth and coordinated movements of the eyes to attend to and follow objects and people in the environment. Controlled eye movements are needed for finding and tracking a moving object, scanning the environment, sustaining eye contact on a fixed object or person, quickly shifting focus from one thing to another, and for eye-hand coordination.

Children with poor ocular control may have difficulty controlling their eyes to follow moving objects. Eye contact, while speaking to another person or fixating the eyes on a task, may be momentary, making it hard to look at something long enough to process its meaning. Children may not be able to copy assignments from the blackboard to the paper in a reasonable amount of time. They may be unable to coordinate smooth eye movements to read across a line. They may have trouble using their eyes to guide their hands for writing and using tools. The children may try to work with their eyes very close to the paper in an effort to gain better ocular control. They also may have problems with depth perception if their eyes are not working well together.

Ocular control is refined developmentally as children are involved in movement activities such as rolling, crawling, and walking in efforts to reach people and objects. Ocular control is challenged when children visually focus on their work or track and locate objects in play. Ocular control is strengthened when children use their eyes to guide and anticipate movement. Three-dimensional play such as throwing and catching, obstacle courses, hopscotch, and playing in relation to targets, baskets, and start and finish lines is valuable in increasing ocular control.

Oral Motor Skills

Oral motor refers to the use of muscles in and around the mouth and cheeks, including the lips and tongue. Motor control of the oral region is necessary for eating, speaking, swallowing, and facial expression. Sensory awareness of the face, lips, cheeks, and tongue, and the integration of touch information are important factors in the development of motor coordination and functional use of the oral area.

Children with poor oral motor control may display a variety of traits. They may drool, lacking adequate lip closure and tongue control. Simple automatic tasks such as chewing and swallowing may be a problem. Oral motor control plays a vital role in the articulation of words and sounds. Without good oral motor skills, children may have difficulty expressing themselves and may even have unusual facial expressions.

The muscles in and around the mouth and face develop naturally as an infant sucks and chews on objects and learns to eat a variety of food textures. As language develops, a wider range of speech sounds emerge, challenging the development of precise lip, cheek, and tongue control. Typical childhood play activities, such as 1-year olds' habit of chewing on toys, stimulate oral motor awareness. There are many sensory nerve endings in the oral motor area that provide the brain with important information regarding size, shape, and texture. Babbling and silly songs help exercise and coordinate the face, tongue, lip, and jaw muscles. Toddlers are often fascinated with the oral motor ability to blow and control their own airflow. Blowing kisses, straws, harmonicas, pinwheels, and party toys further develops oral motor coordination.

If a teacher suspects a child has an oral motor problem, a speech therapist or an occupational therapist should be consulted. Children with oral motor irregularities also may have abnormal reflexes that stimulate a swallow before food can be properly chewed. In general, teachers should ban peanuts in preschool classrooms and should be very careful with popcorn and other food items that do not dissolve easily.

Perception of Movement

Perception of movement refers to the processing of vestibular information in the brain. The receptors in the inner ear perceive information about the force of gravity and movement. By sending messages to higher centers in the brain, the vestibular system aids in maintaining joint stability, posture, balance, motor control, spatial awareness, and a stable visual field. In addition, the vestibular system sends information to a part of the brain that regulates attention. Therefore, movement can be used to facilitate attention or to provide a calming effect.

Some children may not process enough information about gravity and movement, while others "overprocess" the incoming sensory information. Children who are not processing enough movement information may have trouble stabilizing and coordinating neck and eye musculature in order to copy letters, draw, or follow a line in reading. They may not be able to maintain posture subconsciously and may need to concentrate on sitting in chairs. They may lean heavily on a desk when trying to listen to the teacher. When standing in line, they may look for someone or something to lean on. They may lose balance easily or appear to move excessively, using momentum to compensate for poor equilibrium responses.

Children who perceive too much movement information may be overly frightened by movement. They may not be able to keep up with peers on the playground and may have difficulty mastering environmental obstacles such as stairs or uneven terrain. They may become fearful or resistant and refuse to participate in classroom activities. Other children who have low thresholds for tolerating movement may seek too much movement and experience very disorganized behavior after small amounts of stimulation in play.

Many activities provide opportunities for processing and integrating movement information in the brain. Some examples are rocking, rolling, running, hopping, bouncing, skipping, and jumping. Playground equipment such as swings, slides, merry-go-rounds, and teeter-totters are good sources of movement experiences. When a teacher observes that a child is having problems with posture, balance, or tolerating movement, providing these opportunities may be helpful.

If a child appears to fear or seek an excess of movement and this behavior is interfering with independent functioning in the classroom, an occupational therapist should be contacted. A child should never be forced to participate if a problem is suspected. It is important to be sensitive to the movement needs of children and to keep a sharp eye on how children tolerate movement. Some children do not have the ability to communicate effectively and cannot indicate when they have had enough. Passive movement stimulation (in which the child is not able to start and stop the stimulation) is rarely a good idea in the classroom. For example, it is important for a child to be able to put a foot or hand on the ground in order to stop the movement and be in control.

Perception of Touch

Tactile perception pertains to the sense of touch on the skin. The tactile system is a two-fold system involving the interpretation of protective and discriminative information. The protective tactile system is responsible for the body automatically withdrawing or defending itself from touch that is interpreted as harmful. The discriminative touch system provides the brain with the precise information regarding size, shape, and texture of objects in the environment. The integrity of both tactile systems is essential for tool use, eating, speaking and many aspects of social and emotional development.

Children with problems related to a tactile system disorder may be hypersensitive or hyposensitive to touch or have poor tactile discrimination. Hypersensitive children may appear aggressive in their interaction with others. They may avoid art projects or outdoor play in the grass, dirt, or sand because of tactile discomfort. The need to protect themselves from inadvertent tactile input may result in poor attentional skills and poor peer relationships. Hyposensitive children may be unaware of being touched and not react to painful experiences such as cuts and bruises. Children with poor tactile discrimination may have difficulty manipulating tools and toys because they cannot effectively feel and interpret the tactile detail.

Activities providing tactile input include eating, dressing, participating in a variety of art projects, and playing in the grass, sand, water, or dirt. These types of activities give children the opportunity to process and integrate tactile information from the environment. Tactile activities should never be forcibly imposed upon a child who avoids or complains about tactile stimuli. If the teacher suspects that a tactile problem is interfering with tool use, peer relationships, or independent functioning in the classroom, an occupational therapist should be consulted.

Visual-Spatial Perception

Visual-spatial perception is how people perceive the relationship of external space to their bodies, as well as how they perceive objects in space relative to other objects. The importance of eyesight in classroom performance is obvious, but sight alone is not enough. Vision needs to be combined with an interpretation of the physical environment to make sense of what we see.

Visual-spatial perception provides us with important information about our environment. The way children perceive space and their own orientation within that space can affect many aspects of their lives. Students with poor visual perceptual abilities may have difficulty finding their way around the neighborhood or school. The organization of personal belongings ranging from clothing at home to notebooks at school may seem impossible. Understanding certain mathematical concepts and creating strategies in sports and games also can be a problem. Visual-spatial deficits can seriously impact written communication. A student with a disability in this area may not know where to start writing on the paper. Letters may vary in size, spacing and alignment to the point where words, phrases, paragraphs and important thoughts cannot be read. Copying from the chalkboard may be very time consuming as the student is asked to process visual-spatial information across two planes.

Locomotion and mobility provide children with the opportunity to learn about the physical world. As children explore the space around them, their senses of touch, movement, body awareness, and visual input come together to form a sense of relationship between themselves, objects, and space. Initially, visual-spatial perception develops as children move over, under, through, and around objects in the course of play. As these experiences are organized in the brain, perception of form constancy, position of objects in space, figure-ground, and depth begin to emerge. The ability to place cognitive labels on space such as right, left, above, and below is related to children's physical experiences.

Many activities help develop spatial perception. Playgrounds with climbing areas and slides help develop a sense of how one's body relates to space. Activities such as tossing and catching; using targets; playing games with designated boundaries such as hopscotch, four square, and relays; and playing games with bases, baskets, and goals all help to integrate information related to spatial perception. Manipulative toys and art projects provide opportunities to develop visual-spatial strategies that can be used to encourage the precision needed for fine motor work, written communication, and later, an occupation.

Troubleshooting

Sensory and Motor Factors in the Classroom

Children come to school with a wide variety of strengths and limitations. When an assignment is presented to a class of children, there will be many different approaches used in attempting to complete it. Some children will begin and complete a task with ease. Some children will have difficulty staying in their seats or knowing where to begin the task. Other children readily begin an assignment, struggle through it, and never seem to finish. It is the responsibility of the teacher and school district staff to modify activities so that each child experiences success in beginning and completing tasks appropriate for his or her potential with the least amount of frustration and stress.

Modifying an activity is not easy. Many factors contribute to successful performance. The accurate perception of movement, touch, body awareness, auditory and visual information, the coordination of eye movements, the coordination of the two body sides, and the execution of a motor plan all influence a child's ability to perform skillfully without undue effort. The amount of structure provided in the implementation of an activity also can influence the productivity of a class. Positive peer interaction and good sportsmanship further contribute to the success of many activities in the classroom.

Classroom activities can be modified in a number of ways to correspond to a child's sensory and motor needs. The following pages provide strategies that are designed to stimulate a teacher's interest and ability to modify activities.

Strategies for Modifying Activities

When a child is having difficulty with an activity, have you tried . . .

◆ Weighing the value of that activity? Is it something that children really need to master or can they get through school years without this skill?

◆ Practicing activities with similar demands using other media? Try practicing direction-following, listening, independent planning, sequencing, task persistence, and task completion through art projects, music, games, and motor activities.

◆ Following developmental progressions? Consult your favorite developmental schedule or evaluation tool to get ideas for adjusting the expected level of skill.

◆ Progressing from repetition to trial-and-error experimentation to abstract problem-solving? Sometimes children need more time for repetition and experimentation.

◆ Assigning a task that can be completed in a short period of time? Emphasize the completion of a task. Some children have difficulty independently organizing and relating the parts of the whole task. Try to break the task into parts and document success in completing each part. It is more satisfying to complete several small tasks than to continuously struggle and never quite complete one long assignment. Some children need to see instant results. Adjust the task so that the child can finish it in a set amount of time. This will develop a sense of accomplishment and confidence in completing tasks.

◆ Identifying the importance of the end product to the child? Sometimes the process of completing a task is more important to the child than the end product. At other times the end product is very important to the child. Satisfaction builds motivation and persistence.

◆ Adding or subtracting sensory information? When analyzing a task, check the environment for auditory, visual, and tactile distractions. Check the activity and increase or decrease the sensory and motor components if necessary.

The following pages provide examples of ways to add or subtract sensory information.

BEGINNING AND COMPLETING TASKS

Problems in this area could be related to:

Have you tried . . .

Auditory Processing

Difficulty hearing and understanding the spoken word can interfere with a child's ability to begin and complete a task.

◆ Giving one direction at a time? Sometimes, a child who is given a three-part command will act on only the first or last direction.

◆ Using short, simple, one-concept phrases to give directions? Do not elaborate. Repeat verbal directions slowly, firmly, and clearly.

◆ Waiting? Wait a little longer than you think is necessary to give the child time to analyze the command and put it into action.

◆ Giving a visual demonstration or physical assistance?

◆ Reducing auditory distractions? Be aware of papers shuffling, pencils dropping, and so on. Provide earplugs or headphones.

◆ Scheduling classroom activities with high auditory processing demands at a time when auditory competition outside is at a minimum?

◆ Practicing verbal direction-following in gross motor games? Progress from one-step to four-step sequences.

◆ Insisting that a child does not move until you have finished the directions? Have the child repeat the direction in the proper sequence.

Motor Planning

The ability to plan, organize, and sequence strategies is essential to beginning and completing tasks.

◆ Helping the child identify steps needed to begin and accomplish the task? Have the child repeat directions, and if possible, write down or tape-record the steps.

◆ Giving a short assignment so that a child can feel instant success in completing a task? Document the length of time a child can focus on one task and structure the assignment so that it can be completed in that length of time. Try a sand timer to pace work.

◆ A system for checking off steps as they are completed?

◆ Helping the child physically move through the action?

◆ Minimizing visual distractions? Check for clutter in the classroom environment. Provide a study carrel.

◆ Art projects that require assembling parts to create an object? This challenges the child's ability to develop strategies for organizing parts as they relate to the whole.

◆ Playing *Simon Says* and games that require visual imitation to see if the student is able to process directions and copy?

COPYING FROM CHALKBOARD

Problems in this area could be related to:

Ocular Control

Weak eye muscles can tire easily when they are required to repeatedly shift focus from the chalkboard to the desk.

Have you tried . . .

◆ Writing small amounts on the chalkboard at a time?

◆ Alternating chalkboard activities with less visually demanding tasks?

◆ Scheduling a few moments to close and relax eyes between tasks?

◆ Eye-tracking activities such as a suspended ball, balloon, and beanbag games? These games challenge the alternation of focus from near to far. Try to have the target about the same distance as a chalkboard is to a seat.

◆ Wheelbarrow walking and rolling games? These activities help strengthen eye, head, and neck stability important for a stable visual field.

◆ Checking for dull or flickering lights?

◆ Eliminating art objects that dangle from the ceiling? Movement can be distracting and can interfere with the processing of visual information.

Visual-Spatial Perception

Unidentified acuity problems as well as difficulty transferring visual-spatial information across two visual planes can make copying from the chalkboard difficult.

◆ Writing on a board or desk slanted at approximately 30°?

◆ Positioning the child directly in front of the material to be copied?

◆ Checking with parents and the school nurse to see if there is an acuity problem?

◆ Cleaning the chalkboard? Yellow chalk is thought to have the best visibility.

◆ Presenting a lesson using an easel with large white paper and thick, dark, magic markers?

◆ Using an overhead projector so that you can visually isolate different words or sentences?

◆ Copying from one paper to another in the same plane?

◆ Providing the child with an outline of material to be covered on the chalkboard? Until a child is copying independently, try having portions of chalkboard material already on the paper.

◆ Reducing the amount of copying expected? The time it takes for some children to copy compromises the time that they could spend thinking and responding. Provide photocopies of material that would otherwise have to be copied by hand.

◆ Teaching strategies for remembering whole words, phrases, or sentences at one glance? Sometimes copying is done in a tedious letter-by-letter manner.

Problems in this area could be related to:

Coordinating Body Sides

Cutting with scissors requires one hand to guide while the other hand cuts. Both hands must work well together.

Have you tried . . .

♦ Providing opportunities for the right and left arms and hands to work together? Try clapping, catching and throwing, and lummi and rhythm stick games.

♦ Providing opportunities for hands and fingers to practice working together? Try Lego®, pop bead, Tinkertoy®, bead stringing, sewing, and woodworking projects.

♦ Paper folding and paper tearing as part of art projects?

♦ Mixing bowl activities in which one hand stabilizes the bowl and the other hand mixes? Try sand and water or food mixes. For tool variation, try a spoon, whip, egg beater, and fork.

Fine Motor Control

A tool is only as accurate as the hands and fingers that control it. Cutting with scissors requires the ability to move the thumb independently of the fingers.

♦ Hand-grasp strengthening activities? For example, climbing, holding on to the ropes of swings, playing tug-of-war, using a hole punch, and spraying with trigger-type spray bottles can help strengthen grasp.

♦ Providing opportunities for practicing timed grasp and release with tools other than scissors? Try using tweezers or tongs to sort cotton balls, modeling clay, or lentils.

♦ Making sure that the child is guiding the scissors from the base of the blade rather than the tip?

♦ Cutting without concern for precision? Try cutting pieces of straws, grass, strips of paper, or rolls of play dough.

♦ Cutting on $\frac{1}{2}$ inch-wide line?

♦ Adjusting the assignment to the developmental level of the child? Hand movements essential for snipping with scissors emerge at about 18 months. Developmentally, however, children are not ready for scissors until about 5 years of age.

Tool Choice

Scissors come in a variety of sizes and styles.

♦ Scissors that are the proper size for the child's hand? Fingers should be secure in the handle openings.

♦ Scissors that have a short blade?

♦ The proper scissors grasp? The thumb should be in the smaller loop on top, the index finger rests above the opposite opening, and depending upon the type of scissors, just the middle finger, or middle, ring, and little fingers, fit into the opening.

♦ Sharp scissors?

MAINTAINING ORDER IN LINE

Problems in this area could be related to:

Have you tried . . .

Body Awareness

Some children with poor awareness of where, how, and with what force their body parts are moving may inadvertently run into their peers or play too roughly.

- ◆ Markers at the door? Space markers can be made by placing sticker dots or masking tape lines for each child to stand on while waiting.
- ◆ Having young children hold on to a rope with knots spaced 2 feet apart?
- ◆ Allowing extra time and space for children to put on jackets and sweaters prior to getting into line?
- ◆ Complimenting those students who are maintaining order?
- ◆ Allowing students to use a wall for guidance? Some students may feel more organized leaning against the wall.

Visual-Spatial Perception

The interpretation of spatial relationships is sometimes difficult when a child is in motion, walking from one place to another in line.

- ◆ Designating routes to follow? Sometimes there are lines in the cement.
- ◆ Stopping every 20–30 feet to get organized?
- ◆ Identifying landmarks for those students who continue to be disoriented?
- ◆ Lining up two abreast in a buddy system? Sometimes this shortens the line and students can be grouped into successful pairs.
- ◆ Talking about expectations in line?

Perception of Touch

Hypersensitivity to touch can make inadvertent human contact painful and disturbing. Inadvertent physical contact may provoke disruptive behavior in some children.

- ◆ Having the child who has a tendency to be disruptive go first or last in line? This will minimize possible tactile contact.
- ◆ Minimizing the time that the children are expected to stand and wait in line?
- ◆ Allowing a child with suspected hypersensitivity to touch to wear a sweater or jacket indoors?

ORGANIZING MOTOR TIME BEHAVIOR

Problems in this area could be related to:

Degree of Structure

Inadequate structure may contribute to a sense of chaos during motor activities.

Have you tried . . .

◆ Reviewing how to play the game and troubleshooting before actually playing it? Tell the class in words and use diagrams on the blackboard if necessary. Have students interact by asking and answering questions prior to beginning the game.

◆ Implementing motor time in the classroom rather than outside? There are fewer distractions inside, and students are more likely to follow classroom rules. It only takes a minute to move desks aside.

◆ Designating a boundary for each child? Try using carpet squares, chalk, or tape.

◆ Marking the boundaries of the game? For example, rope, yarn, masking tape, or chalk can be used to mark a game circle or start and finish lines.

◆ Using signals for control (e.g., two blows of a whistle or a bell to signal "freeze")? Practice *Simon Says* or freeze-type games.

◆ Stopping action between turns to get everyone's attention and regain control?

◆ Giving one direction at a time? For example, try: "Stand on the line." Pause; wait until the class is on the line; "We are going to . . . (one direction)." Pause, and so on.

◆ Scheduling and implementing frequent (daily) motor time so that the students become familiar with behavioral expectations during motor activities?

◆ Working with small groups of children (about 6–8 in a group)? Divide the children by using a coding system (color, number, animal). A facilitator may be needed for each group.

◆ Making a rule for how loose balls and scattered beanbags will be handled? Designate a person to collect items so the class doesn't lose time and organization.

◆ Scheduling a calming, familiar backup game if the structure of a new game fails? Before a new game is discarded, try to alter the structure for future success.

◆ Ignoring disruptive behavior? Do not reward negative behavior with extra focus or attention.

Continued on page 29

Continued from page 28

Problems in this area could be related to:

Broad Range of Skill Levels

Activities that are too easy or too difficult tend to elicit disruptive behavior.

Have you tried . . .

◆ Initially having the entire class play a game at the lower skill level? Observe the more advanced students' sportsmanship, social communication, and cooperation.

◆ Varying expectations? In target games the size and distance of the target can be varied for each child; and in throw and catch games, the students can be paired high skill with high skill or alternated high skill/low skill.

◆ Complimenting and recognizing the children for cooperation? For example, compliment the student who is at the higher level, "I like the way you are helping Johnny." At the same time, recognize the student at the lower level, "Nice try, John."

◆ Allowing a different number of turns for each child depending on skill level?

◆ Considering ways to make the game easier or more difficult prior to the activity?

◆ Integrating children from other classrooms with similar skill levels?

◆ Dividing into groups (one group per adult) to practice at various skill levels?

◆ Allowing children who are having difficulty 10–15 minutes of extra practice time, possibly at recess?

ORGANIZING PERSONAL BELONGINGS

Problems in this area could be related to:

Body Awareness

Inaccurate awareness of where, how, and with what force body parts are moving in relation to objects can cause personal belongings to be disorganized.

Visual-Spatial Perception

Difficulty with figure-ground perception (identifying objects with a rival background) can contribute to problems with sorting and organizing personal belongings.

Have you tried . . .

◆ Stabilizing school supplies by weighting the child's pencil box and other containers? Use washers or plaster of paris.

◆ Triangular finger grips on pencils and crayons to prevent them from rolling off the desk?

◆ A clipboard and large bulldog clips to keep papers together?

◆ Taping a line across double desks to designate individual space?

◆ Keeping only necessary items on desktops?

◆ Allowing a limited number of personal belongings at school?

◆ Designating a place or container for each belonging?

◆ Scheduling a set time each day to organize belongings? Children need extra time to get organized; try to work it into your routine.

◆ A color-coded filing system? Folded construction paper of different colors can signify different subjects or complete and incomplete work.

◆ Discussing strategies for organizing personal belongings? Ideas include talking about similarities and differences between objects, and sorting like objects. This can be applied to cleaning a bedroom, doing the dishes, and sorting collections of rocks, bugs, or sea shells.

◆ Assisting the student by analyzing part-to-whole relationships in how to organize a desk? Minimize the objects in the desk.

◆ Allowing time each week to clean out and organize notebooks, pencil boxes, and books?

◆ Consistent and orderly classroom expectations for where to turn in assignments, keep backpacks, put trash, and so on?

Problems in this area could be related to:

Body Awareness

Deficient strength and tone in the muscles may make it tiring to sit erect for long periods.

Have you tried . . .

◆ Checking for proper child-seat-desk proportions? Feet should rest comfortably on the floor. The table should be a forearm's length away from the chin—that is, with the elbow resting on the table, the fist should fit under the chin.

◆ Placing a heavy beanbag on the child's lap to add resistance and increase body awareness?

◆ Periodically putting firm pressure on a child's shoulders?

◆ Providing a brief period of classroom aerobics? Jumping, running in place, and so on, may be the input children need to stay in their seats for longer periods of time.

◆ Alternating work centers? Try providing a specific place to work where the child can stand, kneel, or lie prone. Expect at least 5 minutes of work at each center.

◆ Beanbag chairs to aid in supporting body weight more comfortably?

◆ Using a table with a cutout for additional side support?

◆ Expecting less erect posture, particularly during academic tasks requiring high concentration and toward the end of the day?

◆ Helping the child physically move through the action?

Perception of Touch

A hypersensitivity to touch may make it difficult for some children to stay in a seat because they are trying to avoid inadvertent touch from the child next to them.

◆ Spacing tactually defensive children in positions so that they are not sitting close enough to touch other children?

◆ Allowing tactually defensive children to wear favorite sweaters or jackets when they are in situations in which they will be near other children?

◆ Spot markers or carpet squares to help designate personal space when sitting on the floor?

◆ Avoiding unpredictable physical contact when assisting the child?

Motor Planning

The ability to plan, organize, and sequence classroom work is an important foundation for attending to tasks and staying in one's seat.

◆ Helping the child identify steps needed to begin and accomplish the task? Have the child repeat directions and, if possible, write down the steps.

◆ Giving a short assignment so that a child can experience instant success in completing a task? Document the length of time a child can focus on one task and structure the assignment so it can be completed in that time. Try a timer to pace work.

◆ A system for checking off steps as they are completed?

◆ Giving one direction at a time? After one action is successfully completed, add another direction.

◆ Art projects that require assembling parts to create an object? This challenges the child's ability to develop strategies for organizing parts as they relate to the whole.

PRODUCING ORGANIZED WRITTEN WORK

Problems in this area could be related to:

Have you tried . . .

Body Awareness

Poor automatic awareness of where, how, and with what force body parts are moving can account for torn or wrinkled work, holes in papers, and broken pencils.

◆ Different writing tools such as regular and wide pencils, mechanical pencils, markers of differing diameters, erasable pens, or colored pencils? Various sizes and shapes of writing tools may provide the correct feedback for control.

◆ A variety of tripod pencil grips? This may help tense children relax their grips, resulting in better control of the amount of pressure used when writing. See the options in the *Classroom Modifications* section of this book.

◆ Providing the child with thicker paper? Try gluing the child's writing paper onto construction paper for extra support.

◆ Playing prewriting warm-up exercises such as wheelbarrow walking, donkey kicks, or tug-of-war? These games "wake-up" some of the stabilizing muscle groups used for good fine motor control.

◆ Pouring exercises? Have the child experiment with trying to pour specified amounts of sand, lentils, rice, or liquid from a cup or pitcher. Strive for accuracy in force of movement. This will help a child learn to modulate or grade the amount of muscle force needed in fine motor work.

◆ Beanbag games using beanbags of different weights and targets of varying distances? These games challenge the muscles to react to where, how, and with what force they are moving.

Visual-Spatial Perception

Inaccurate perception of the relationship of one's body to external space can contribute to a disorganized approach to a task. Faulty interpretation of the spatial relationships of objects, letters, and words to one another also contributes to messy work.

◆ Providing adequate strategies and time to organize and straighten up the work area between activities as part of a daily routine?

◆ Using graph or quadrille paper for math? The boxes make it easy to line up numbers in correct columns.

◆ Emphasizing spatial terms? Use colored tape on the desk. On the left side, use green to show a starting point. On the right side, use red to show a stopping point.

◆ Taping paper to the desk at no more than a 45° angle?

◆ Art projects that require spatial precision?

◆ A shield or folding paper to eliminate visual distractions? Cut a hole in a piece of card stock paper the average size of a word or sentence. This can be placed over the paper a child is working on and moved as needed.

◆ Motor time activities that incorporate precision into movement? Games such as hopscotch challenge precision, accuracy, and working within a defined space.

◆ A craft stick, tongue depressor, or strip of paper to mark spaces between words?

◆ Premarked paper? Try premarking the paper, indicating a space appropriate for the name, date, and subject.

Problems in this area could be related to:

Peer Interaction

Social skills impact how children treat one another. The ability to get along with peers is practiced and challenged in many classroom activities throughout the day. Good peer interaction is a critical life skill. Children with sensory processing problems often act impulsively and in a defensive manner, often offending peers.

Have you tried . . .

◆ A review of the classroom rules? Have the children tell you the rules of the classroom and the game before beginning the activity.

◆ Positive reinforcement techniques? Give immediate, honest, and positive comments on each small effort or appropriate social interaction, such as "I like how you are waiting for your turn," or "That was nice of you to help Johnny."

◆ Ignoring the disruptive behavior while complimenting the desired behavior? "I like the way the red team is lining up. They can be first."

◆ Providing game ideas for structured recess? Leisure time without a plan is problematic for some children.

◆ Avoiding chase-type games? These games lead to chaos.

◆ Providing enough equipment so that everyone can participate within a reasonable amount of time? Try to reduce the time that children spend waiting for a turn.

◆ Dividing teams in advance or varying the method used for choosing sides? Avoid teams chosen by students, unless the method is objective.

◆ A private coaching session with a child who has difficulty interacting with others? Help the child identify times in which he or she reacts with poor social skills. Make the child aware of when and why this occurs. Helping a child develop a sense of self-awareness leads to control over behavior.

◆ Identifying options for a child to use when he or she feels angry? For example, use a good sense of humor, walk away to a safe space, ask the person who is bothering the child to stop, or seek a facilitator such as a teacher.

Perception of Touch

Hypersensitivity to touch can make inadvertent human contact painful or disturbing. Unpredictable physical contact may provoke disruptive behavior in some children.

◆ Allowing the child to wear a favorite sweater or jacket if hypersensitivity to touch is suspected when the child will be near other children and experiencing unpredictable touch?

◆ Markers to designate personal space?

◆ Talking about the game strategy to children who are suspected of being hypersensitive to touch? If appropriate, mention that sometimes other children may accidentally bump into them. This will give children better control and predictability about what will happen to them.

◆ Allowing the hypersensitive child to have more personal space when participating in group activities?

◆ Providing carpet squares when the class is sitting on the grass or concrete?

Continued on page 34

Continued from page 33

Problems in this area could be related to:

Sportsmanship

Sportsmanship includes fair play and the ability to take turns, encourage one another, and to accept wins and losses in play.

Have you tried . . .

◆ Scheduling consistent gross motor, board game, and structured free time to practice sportsmanship? Frequent opportunities with a good facilitator build sportsmanship.

◆ Structuring games so that everyone wins and no one loses? Rules of most traditional games can be changed so that no one is eliminated.

◆ Changing roles frequently in games so that students can experience being leader versus participant, first versus last, and so on?

◆ Adding a cooperative component to dodge ball-type games? For example, have children pass the ball three times before throwing it.

◆ Reviewing how to play the game and troubleshooting before actually playing it? Tell the class in words and use diagrams on the chalkboard if necessary. Have children interact by asking and answering questions prior to the game. This is essential in organizing a successful game and will lead to more fair play.

◆ Appointing a facilitator or referee to kindly point out who is next, who gets the point, and why. Children learn fair play through various conflicts that come up in games and sports. A conflict handled fairly can be a very positive experience.

WRITING WITH PENCILS

Problems in this area could be related to:

Fine Motor Control

A tool is only as accurate as the hands and fingers that control it.

Have you tried . . .

◆ Letting the child practice writing on a vertical surface using the chalkboard, an easel, dry erase board, or paper taped to the wall? This promotes shoulder, elbow, and wrist strength as well as the correct pencil grasp.

◆ Art projects requiring less precise use of pencils and crayons? Try pencil eraser stamping on quadrille paper or rub art with crayons.

◆ Limiting the number of written assignments?

◆ Alllowing typed reports, oral reports, or reports dictated onto a cassette?

◆ Experimenting with various diameters and styles of writing tools? Sometimes smaller diameter tools are easier for little fingers to control.

◆ Adaptive pencil grips?

◆ Discussing the importance of neat penmanship? Sometimes messy handwriting is related to a poor attitude or overall sense of disorganization.

◆ Teaching cursive writing? For some children the flow of cursive writing is easier than printing.

Visual-Spatial Perception and Ocular Motor Control

The correct interpretation of the spatial relationship of objects, letters, and words to one another is essential to legible writing. Coordinated eye movements are important for the eyes to smoothly guide the hands.

◆ Practicing spatial relationships using manipulative toys to duplicate sequences or structures?

◆ Letter formation with finger paint? Try shaving cream on a desk.

◆ Practicing writing letters in the air with streamers?

◆ Writing letters with a paintbrush and water on the cement?

◆ Practicing letters with stencils?

◆ Taping the alphabet to the desktop for easy reference?

◆ Providing a craft stick or paper strip to use as a marker between words as they are written to help the child with proper spacing?

◆ Playing balloon, suspended ball, and beanbag games? Some children need to be reminded to look at and work with the object they are coordinating with their hand.

◆ Using smaller ruled paper? Sometimes it is easier to write smaller.

Classroom
Modifications

The Classroom

Seating Arrangement

It is important to consider the sensory and motor demands placed upon the student when lessons are presented. Consider the physical and visual relationship of the teacher to the student when instructions are presented. Be aware of visual and auditory distractions that may affect your classroom.

Desks and chairs facing the teacher and chalkboard provide consistent forward orientation toward the instruction area. This consistency is very important to children with attention deficits or sensory processing disorders. It also provides a physical space between rows of students that may be helpful in accommodating fidgety students and students who require more predictable tactile and physical space.

Desks placed in various positions in relation to the front of the room require that some students constantly have to turn sideways for instruction. Be aware of where instruction is given and provide forward orientation for all students. In a seating arrangement where four students are sitting around tables placed in a square, the teacher needs to consider teaching and presenting blackboard material from four different instruction areas.

Seating arrangements where two students share a table should be considered with caution. Some students require a larger physical and tactile space. The productivity of both students could be compromised. In some instances, however, this seating arrangement may be a positive experience as one student can serve as a role model or coach for another.

Floors, Bulletin Boards, Countertops, and Desktops

Classroom clutter can be visually distracting to some students. It is important to have the working area well organized. Designate a place to store backpacks, jackets, and lunches. Check to make sure classroom supplies and projects are stored and organized after those valuable periods of creative chaos. Counters and floors should always be clear or at least well organized.

Desk clutter can lead to student disorganization. Have a system in place for storing pencils, crayons, scissors, rulers, and personal belongings. Provide time daily to organize notebooks and papers.

Make it a point to provide color-coded folders, a three-hole punch, staplers, and so on. To assist students in focusing on the activity at hand, only essential materials should be visible and easily accessible.

Blackboard, easels, and overhead projector materials should be checked for visibility for all students. Consider the size, contrast, and visual organization of the material presented.

Classroom Noise

Children spend almost half of the school day in listening activities. Noise created outside the classroom in conjunction with noise generated by a classroom full of students can be challenging for everyone and even overwhelming for some students.

Be aware of the maintenance, lawn mowing, and outside work schedule as well as the auditory effect of other classes in transit upon your classroom. Negotiate a change if it interferes with instruction.

Listen for buzzing fluorescent lights and noisy heaters and air conditioners. Have these serviced as soon as possible and be persistent. It is very distracting for some students to have to deal with this type of background noise.

Classroom Lighting

Classrooms should have adequate lighting throughout. Be aware of burned out lights, flickering lights, and possible glare from sunlight. Flickering lights can be very distracting to some students, and unless identified and eliminated could contribute to significant subconscious sensory irritation and decreased function.

Desk and Chair Proportions

Students spend several hours each day sitting at a desk. To maximize student performance in handwriting, reading, copying from the blackboard, and attending to instruction, a proper fit is essential. Most desks can be raised or lowered, and chairs come in a variety of sizes.

◆ The child should sit so that the back has support and the hips and knees bend at approximately a 90° angle. Feet should rest comfortably on the floor.

◆ The proper desk height should enable the student to place his or her elbow on the writing surface with the fist fitting comfortably under the chin.

Writing Surfaces

It is important to recognize a child's body awareness, fine motor control, and visual-spatial perception in selecting a writing surface. Some children have difficulty copying from one visual plane to another because of perceptual difficulties. Providing a variety of planes and surfaces will help a child develop joint stability, body awareness, and perceptual constancy necessary for learning writing skills during the early grades.

◆ Vertical writing: The classroom chalkboard is a readily available option for writing on a vertical plane. Make sure that the child has a clean surface at eye level on which to work. Taping paper to any smooth wall or surface also will work well. Try attaching a doodle board toy or dry erase board to the wall for additional options. Vertical writing helps develop the muscles that stabilize the shoulder, elbow, and wrist, and it also improves the position of the hand for manipulating a writing tool. Vertical writing helps eliminate visual-spatial confusion that occurs when copying from one visual plane to another. Some children can better complete their assignments in an upright standing posture than when seated.

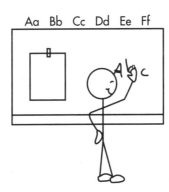

◆ Writing on a slanted surface: The slanted surface is an option that can be used while the child is seated. Adjustable slantboards are available commercially, but a less expensive idea is to place a closed 4″ three-ring binder on the desktop so that it slants toward the child. A clipboard then holds the paper in position. When learning letter formation, many children enjoy holding individual chalkboards or dry erase boards in their lap while seated on the floor. The art easel is another option for writing on a slanted plane.

◆ Writing on a flat surface: Children love to get on hands and knees and draw on concrete with sidewalk chalk. This challenges postural stability and balance. It also is washed away easily with water. Try taping a large sheet of butcher paper to the floor. Children can write and draw while lying on their stomachs. This helps develop postural strength of the neck and back and coordinate head and eye movements.

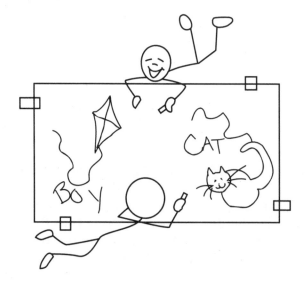

Paper

Paper often is an overlooked component in written work that can be modified easily to meet individual needs. Paper can have boundaries (lines, squares) or no boundaries. Paper can be thin (newsprint) or thick (construction paper). It can make or break the presentation of written work.

Paper Without Boundaries

Plain paper can be modified in a number of ways. Paper comes in different densities. Experiment to find the thickness of paper that produces the best result. Usually, classrooms are issued a standard paper. To modify it, try gluing it to a piece of construction paper or even tag board to make it more sturdy. Sometimes kindergarten and primary paper is too large. Try cutting it into smaller segments to make it more manageable.

When learning to make various shapes and letters, it is important to first have time to practice the basic shape without having to relate it to a line. Practice shapes without border requirements before using borders and lines. Try classroom or individual chalk boards, dry erase boards, or commercial doodle boards.

Writing on a Textured Surface

The practice of drawing letters and numbers in a tactile media can facilitate learning and the automatic kinesthetic and visual retention of specific letter formation. Students have fun using index fingers in media such as shaving cream, finger paint, sand, and pudding.

Simulated Paper

Lines can be drawn on the cement with chalk and cut-out letters can be used to spell words with correct spacing and correct orientation to

Chalk on concrete

the line. Games can be played in which scores are kept for proper placement and orientation to the line. Children can progress to using chalk or paintbrushes with water to write on the cement within the proper boundaries.

Use tape or hook and loop strips to make boundary lines on the floor or carpet and have the children place blocks with letters in the appropriate position.

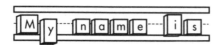

Blocks spaced on taped lines

Children need to develop awareness of their bodies as they relate to boundaries. This is a foundation for visually relating to boundaries on paper. Gross motor games such as hopscotch and four square challenge a child to become aware of concepts such as *inside the line, on the line,* and *outside the line.* Fine motor games such as coloring, tracing, and adhering stickers to a precise shape are beneficial in developing this skill.

Stickers on a shape

Magnetic tape can be used to make lines on cookie sheets or metal surfaces. Children can place magnetic letters, shapes, or numerals between the lines.

Lined Paper

To begin working within borders, use unlined paper folded into squares or in a horizontal fan shape to produce lines. Simple art projects, patterns, drawings, or even letters can be made within the boundaries.

There is a wide variation in lined paper, ranging from a 1-inch line divided into $\frac{1}{2}$-inch areas for upper- and lowercase, to a $\frac{1}{2}$-inch writing space. Traditionally, students in kindergarten are given very wide ruled paper. If a student has trouble using this space, try using second- or third-grade paper with smaller spaces.

Elementary school line paper is coded. Students sometimes have trouble learning to work within these boundaries. There is usually a writing space divided by a dotted line for upper- and lowercase and a narrow line between each set of lines. Sometimes it is helpful to spend time working with what is expected with the lines before actually beginning penmanship. For example, the in-between lines can be colored, producing striped paper. This will accentuate the two lines in which the child is expected to write. Having this visual impact will assist a student in knowing what is expected prior to motorically trying the master the lines.

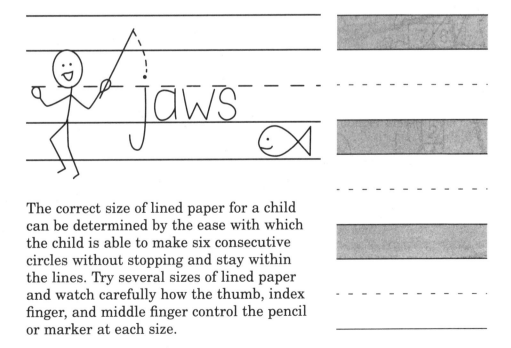

The correct size of lined paper for a child can be determined by the ease with which the child is able to make six consecutive circles without stopping and stay within the lines. Try several sizes of lined paper and watch carefully how the thumb, index finger, and middle finger control the pencil or marker at each size.

Paper that has raised lines to produce kinesthetic feedback can be made or purchased. String can be glued onto the lines of regular school paper, glued to construction paper or tagboard, and laminated. Children then can use wipe-off erasable pencils to practice writing and will feel the line. String also can be dipped in wax, dried, and used on any surface to act as a kinesthetic border.

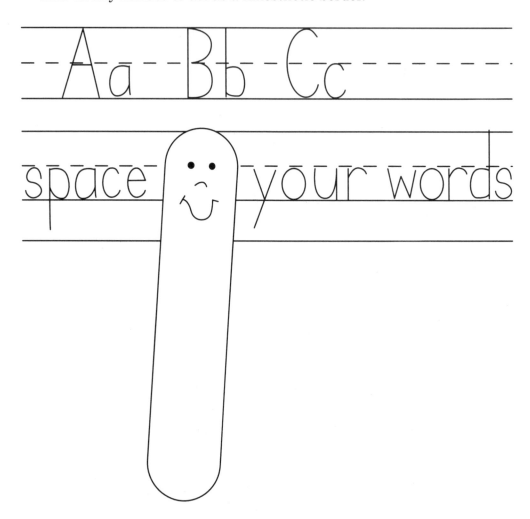

Craft sticks or strips of thick paper can be used to measure the spacing between words by placing them at the end of each word.

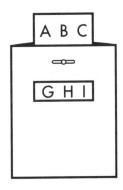

Paper shields can be used to help isolate and organize visual space. Depending upon the size and type of shield needed, a letter-sized envelope or a manilla envelope can be used. An opening is created at the top and bottom of the envelope, one or more windows are cut, and paper can be inserted into the envelope.

Quadrille paper can be used to help develop awareness of the letter or number spacing. This is a valuable modification to use in aligning math columns and even words in a sentence. Quadrille or graph paper comes in $1/4$-inch, $1/2$-inch, and 1-inch squares.

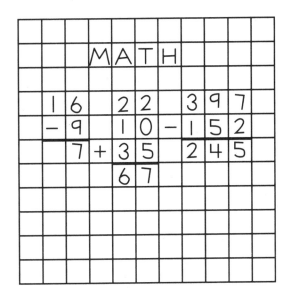

Writing Tools

Writing tools include fingers, chalk, wooden styli, paintbrushes, pencils, pens, marking pens, and computer keyboards. The modifications and variations are endless.

Size

Chalk, paintbrushes, pencils, grease pencils, pens, and markers come in a variety of diameters and lengths. Consider trying wide-diameter writing tools and tools with narrow diameters. Traditionally, kindergarten students are given fat crayons and pencils. Sometimes this is good and provides the student with a substantial tool to hold, feel, and control. Other times the big crayons and pencils are hard to manage and make it difficult to stay in lines and write with precision.

The diameter of a writing tool can be modified with a variety of pencil grips, foam tubing, and even wooden beads. It is important to take the time to observe work samples and student effort to determine whether these modifications are beneficial.

Short pencils can be used for students who have difficulty holding a pencil properly. This requires that the student hold the pencil closer to the point, which may promote the adaptive response of a better tripod grasp and approach.

Point

The point or nib of the writing tool can facilitate or hinder the flow and precision of the written work. The point or writing surface of the chalk, paintbrush, pencil, pen, or marker can be wide or very fine. There also is a variation in resistance as the writing tool comes into contact with the paper. Some tools flow easily, such as paintbrushes and marking pens. Dry markers, grease pencils, and chalk offer increased resistance.

Weight

Pencils, pens, and other writing tools can sometimes be weighted to add tactile and muscular feedback from the hands. Be cautious when using weights, because a too heavy instrument can cause poor compensation in grasp and undue fatigue. A variety of weighted pens are available commercially.

Ball and Balloon Games

Ball and Balloon Games

Primary Sensory and Motor Components Challenged in Each Activity

	AUDITORY PROCESSING	BODY AWARENESS	COORDINATING BODY SIDES	FINE MOTOR	MOTOR PLANNING	OCULAR CONTROL	ORAL MOTOR SKILLS	PERCEPTION OF MOVEMENT	PERCEPTION OF TOUCH	VISUAL-SPATIAL PERCEPTION
Balloon Volley	◆				◆	◆				
Bucket Ball		◆								◆
Bunt Baseball			◆			◆			◆	
Center Stride Ball					◆			◆		
Circle Relay	◆	◆								
Crab-Walk Soccer					◆			◆		
Foot Volley					◆			◆		
Four Square		◆			◆					
Kanga Ball			◆		◆					◆
Marble Ball					◆	◆				
Punchball					◆					
Suspended Ball					◆	◆				
Target Soccer		◆			◆					

Balloon Volley

Equipment

Large round balloon—one for every group of five to seven children
Cloth-covered balloon
Gertie® ball (pliable balloon type of ball)
Beach ball
Nerf® ball

Activity

Form a group of five to seven children in a circle. Stand in the center of the circle and, one child at a time, toss the balloon to each child. Ask the children to hit or catch the balloon using both hands and to avoid being hit in the chest. A line of yarn can be tied to the balloon so that the balloon can be retrieved if the child misses—this helps to add control and structure to the activity. The children can try to hit the balloon or ball using two hands together, the left hand, the right hand, the head, the elbow, and so on.

For variation, have one of the children stand in the center of the circle and toss the balloon to a child that you name. The children are encouraged to watch the balloon and clap when the named child hits or catches it.

Volleyball/Tennis: Try volleying and catching the balloon or ball across a low volleyball net. A "net" can be made by tying a jump rope between two chairs. Divide the class into two teams. Have the students catch the balloon or ball until they get the hang of the game, then have the children try volleying with a two-handed bat (see Appendix A), a table tennis paddle, or a shortened tennis racquet.

This activity works better indoors.

Teacher Observations

Auditory Processing: Can the child follow the verbal command when given?

Motor Planning: Can the child anticipate and make appropriate changes in body position to hit the balloon or ball?

Ocular Control: Can the child visually pursue the balloon or ball?

Bucket Ball

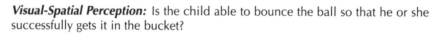

Equipment

Tennis balls—one for each child plus four extra balls
Large, deep bucket or wastebasket

Activity

The children form a large circle and the bucket is placed in the center. Give each child a tennis ball. When a child's name is called, he or she tries to bounce the ball into the bucket. Each time the child succeeds, he or she gets another chance. If the ball bounces out of the bucket, it is counted as a successful attempt, and the child continues to play. Once a child misses the bucket, another child's name is called, and that child takes a turn.

Teacher Observations

Body Awareness: Does the child use sufficient force to successfully bounce the ball into the bucket?

Visual-Spatial Perception: Is the child able to bounce the ball so that he or she successfully gets it in the bucket?

Bunt Baseball

Equipment

Two-handed bottle bat (see Appendix A)
Nerf® or lightweight ball, about 9 inches
Base markers—one for each child

Activity

Group the players onto a pie-shaped field. The catcher, batter, and pitcher are aligned in the traditional manner. The remaining children stand behind a base marker in a semicircle behind the pitcher. The child up to bat grasps the two-handed bat at each end and attempts to bunt the ball. After the ball is hit, the closest baseman catches or retrieves it and throws it to the pitcher. The ball is then thrown from one baseman to the next around the semicircle and back to the pitcher. The batter's objective is to "run" all the bases and reach home before the ball has returned to the pitcher.

This activity can be varied by having the batter hop, jump, run backwards, and so on, while rounding the bases. The basemen can vary how they pass the ball by throwing it two-handed, overhand, through the legs, or bouncing it. If the children have difficulty understanding the concept of the game, it may need to be simplified by practicing each step separately.

Teacher Observations

Coordinating Body Sides: Can the child coordinate both hands together when bunting with the bat?

Ocular Control: Does the child track the ball in flight and effectively position his or her body to catch it?

Visual-Spatial Perception: Is the child able to judge the direction and distance to the other children when throwing the ball?

Center Stride Ball

Equipment

Playground ball

Activity

The children form a circle standing with their feet apart. Their shoes should be touching those of the children positioned on each side of them. Each child attempts to roll the ball through the legs of another child or to block the ball, using his or her hands as it is rolled toward him or her. If the ball passes through the child's legs, that child retrieves the ball and returns it to play. The goal is to complete the game without allowing the ball to go between one's legs.

Teacher Observations

Motor Planning: Is the child able to effectively direct the ball? Is the child able to consistently block the shot?

Perception of Movement: Is the child able to maintain balance while bending and changing his or her center of gravity?

54   Ball and Balloon Games

Circle Relay

Equipment

Kick ball

Activity

The children stand in a circle, arms-length apart, facing their neighbors' backs. A ball is given to one of the children who then begins to pass it overhead, or between the legs to the child behind him or her. The ball continues to be passed around the circle in this manner.

To vary the activity, the teacher may designate a repeated pattern to follow as the ball is passed. For example, three children pass the ball over their heads, then two children pass the ball between their knees, and the pattern is repeated.

The children also may face the center of the circle and pass the ball in a designated pattern. You may incorporate bouncing, catching, or dribbling.

Teacher Observations

Auditory Processing: Are the children able to follow the verbal directions?

Body Awareness: Are the children able to position themselves so they can pass the ball to the children behind them?

Crab-Walk Soccer

Equipment

Ball—punchball, beach ball, or playground ball
Masking tape, chalk line, or boxes for goals

Activity

Children divide equally into two teams. Goals are set up approximately ten feet apart. The children assume a "crab-walk" position and the ball is thrown into the center. Each side tries to get the ball to their goal by bumping it with their bodies or kicking it with their feet. Hands may not be used.

Teacher Observations

Motor Planning: Can the child move forward, backward, and sideways? Does the child easily change direction of movement?

Ocular Control: Does the child maintain visual contact with the ball?

Perception of Movement: Can the child maintain his or her balance while lifting a leg to kick without falling?

Foot Volley

Equipment

Beach ball or punchball—one for every group of four to six children

Activity

The children sit in a circle and propel the ball from one to another by kicking it. When the ball goes out of the circle, the child retrieving it must grasp it, using his or her feet. Hands may not be used. To maintain order, have the child with the ball volley it to another child that the teacher names.

For variation, switch from volleying to passing the ball around the circle with the feet, elbows, wrists, or hands. Try combinations of elbow/knee, hand/foot, and so on for holding the ball.

Teacher Observations

Motor Planning: Can the child direct the flight of the ball with his or her feet? Can the child assume the various body positions required to pass the ball, using a combination of body parts?

Perception of Movement: Can the child maintain his or her balance while sitting and kicking the ball?

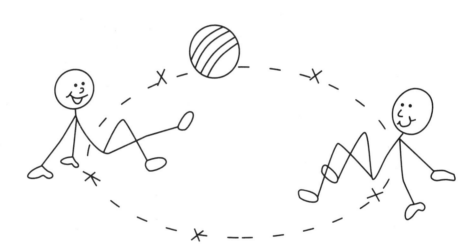

Four Square

Equipment

Playground ball—one for every group of six to eight children
Chalk

Activity

Draw an eight foot by eight foot square on the playground or a paved area. Divide the square into four equal boxes and label each box where they intersect as box A, B, C, and D. Select one student to stand in each square, with the remaining children in line near the D square. The game begins when the child in box A tosses the ball to the child in box B. The child in box B tosses the ball to the child in box C, and so on. The children remain in the boxes until one child fouls out. If a child tosses the ball out of the box or on a line, he or she is out and goes to the end of the line of waiting children. If a child does not catch the ball, he or she is out. When a child fouls, that child goes to the end of the line and the remaining students move up the alphabet. For example, D moves to C, B moves to A, and the first child in line would occupy the D square.

For variation, use different balls or identify different methods of throwing and catching. For example, try passing the ball with and without a bounce. Older students may be able to play without catching the ball each time, by controlling the bounce to the next square.

Teacher Observations

Body Awareness: Is the student able to stay in the proper square and work within the boundaries?

Motor Planning: Is the child able to move his or her body to anticipate the ball? Can he or she plan and deliver tosses to land in the appropriate box?

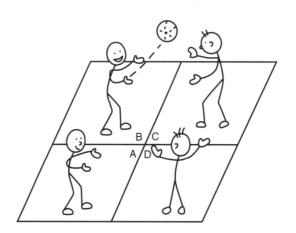

Kanga Ball

Equipment

Tennis balls or kick balls—one for every group of three children

Activity

Divide the children into groups of three. Two of the children sit 10 to 15 feet apart, facing each other. The third child stands with legs apart, halfway between the two children. The children who are seated are given a ball to roll back and forth between the middle child's legs. After six successful rolls, the children change places.

To vary this activity, the child in the middle may be asked to jump a half or a whole turn over the ball as it rolls under his or her feet.

The number of children standing in the center can be varied. With each successful roll of the ball, another child can be added to straddle the center until as many children as possible stand in the center, forming a tunnel for the ball.

Teacher Observations

Coordinating Body Sides: Is the child able to exert even pressure with both hands when pushing the ball?

Motor Planning: With each attempt, does the child learn to more accurately direct the ball?

Visual-Spatial Perception: Does the child visually align the ball before rolling it?

Marble Ball

Equipment

Tennis balls—two for every child

Activity

The children sit on the floor and form a closed circle with their legs apart and feet touching. Give each child one tennis ball. Place the remaining balls in the center of the circle, scattering them. The object of the game is to hit the tennis balls into the center of the circle—similar to playing marbles. The children may keep any of the tennis balls that come within arm's reach. The tennis balls may be redistributed as needed.

To vary the activity, have two children roll their tennis balls across to one another without hitting any of the balls in the middle of the circle.

For another variation, have the children take turns trying to make two balls collide.

Teacher Observations

Motor Planning: Is the child able to accurately direct the roll of the tennis ball?

Ocular Control: Does the child sustain visual contact with the target as he or she rolls the ball?

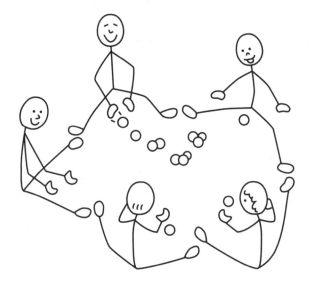

Punchball

Equipment

Playground ball

Activity

Children scatter to form an outfield, with one child in the batter's position. No bases or pitchers are needed. The batter must bounce the ball and then hit it with both hands held together. The outfielder who catches the ball then changes places with the batter.

To increase the challenge, have the batter designate the direction the ball will be hit.

Teacher Observations

Motor Planning: Can the child bounce the ball and successfully time the hit? Can the child control the direction that the ball is hit?

Suspended Ball

Equipment

Suspended ball or balloon—one for every group of two to four children
Two-handed bottle bat—one for each suspended ball (see Appendix A)
Targets—stickers, colored shapes, letters, or numerals
Beanbags

Activity

Suspend the ball at the child's shoulder level. The child sits, lies, kneels, or stands and hits the ball with his or her hands, fingers, elbows, knees, or head. To easily accommodate hitting the ball from different positions, set up stations with balls suspended at various heights.

Swing the ball to the child and have him or her catch it with the right hand, left hand, or with both hands. The child can hit the suspended ball with a two-handed bottle bat, paper towel roll, or wrapping paper roll.

Targets can be placed on the suspended ball. The child is asked to look at and hit the target as the ball moves.

Have the child throw beanbags at the suspended ball.

Teacher Observations

Motor Planning: Does the child anticipate and make appropriate changes in body position in order to hit the target?

Ocular Control: Can the child visually track the moving ball?

Target Soccer

Equipment

Soft playground ball
Three weighted plastic pop bottles (see Appendix A)
One 2′ × 4′ target area—taped off

Activity

The three pop bottles are spaced evenly apart 2 feet behind the target area. The children line up about 15 feet from the center of the target area and take turns kicking the ball at the bottles. One child plays the goalie. The goalie stands in the target area and stops the ball from hitting any of the bottles. The goalie may not step outside the taped boundary or use his or her hands.

Teacher Observations

Body Awareness: Does the child use an appropriate amount of force to propel the ball?

Motor Planning: Is the child able to time kicks accurately?

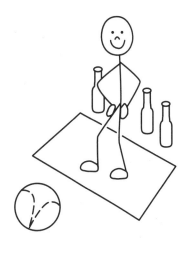

Beanbag Games

Beanbag Games

Primary Sensory and Motor Components Challenged in Each Activity

	AUDITORY PROCESSING	BODY AWARENESS	COORDINATING BODY SIDES	FINE MOTOR	MOTOR PLANNING	OCULAR CONTROL	ORAL MOTOR SKILLS	PERCEPTION OF MOVEMENT	PERCEPTION OF TOUCH	VISUAL-SPATIAL PERCEPTION
Animal-Walk Bowling		◆			◆	◆				
Beanbag Balance					◆			◆		
Beanbag Catch					◆	◆				
Beanbag Pass			◆		◆					
Beanbag Sequence	◆				◆					
Beanbag Target		◆			◆					◆
Beanbags in a Basket	◆	◆								
Toss Across		◆								◆
Toss at a Rolling Ball					◆	◆				
Toss at a Target		◆				◆				
Toss, Jump, Pick Up								◆		◆
Turtle Races		◆							◆	

Animal-Walk Bowling

Equipment

Beanbags—one for each group of three to four children
Weighted plastic pop bottle—one for each group of three to four children (see Appendix A)
Start and throw lines, 12–15 feet apart—masking tape may be used

Activity

Groups of three to four children line up in teams relay style on the start line. The first child in each group animal-walks to the throw line where he or she picks up a beanbag and throws it at the weighted plastic pop bottles, attempting to knock them over. The child then animal-walks back to his or her team and goes to the end of the line. The teacher or a designated child sets up the pop bottles and returns the beanbags to the throw line.

Vary the distance between the throw line and the target. Adjust the level of competition from basic target practice to score-keeping.

Teacher Observations

Body Awareness: Can the child maintain the animal-walk position while moving?

Motor Planning: Can the child assume the animal-walk position and sequence the steps required?

Ocular Control: Does the child make visual contact with the target while throwing?

Beanbag Balance

Equipment

Beanbags—one for each group of two to three children
Start and finish lines, 12–14 feet apart—masking tape or chalk may be used

Activity

Groups of two to three children line up relay style on the start line. The first child in each group assumes an animal-walk posture and balances a beanbag on a designated part of his or her body. The child then attempts to carry the beanbag without dropping it while animal-walking to the finish line. Should the child drop the beanbag, he or she must start over. If the child drops it a second time, he or she repositions the beanbag and continues to the finish line. Once the child reaches the finish line, he or she throws the beanbag to the next child on the team, who is waiting at the start line.

The weight and size of the beanbags may vary; a heavier beanbag may be easier to balance.

Teacher Observations

Motor Planning: Can the child perform the designated variety of movements?

Perception of Movement: Does the child make adequate adjustments to balance the beanbag?

Beanbag Catch

Equipment

Beanbags—one for each child

Activity

Instruct the children in the following activities:

◆ Throw the beanbag up in the air and catch it when it comes down.
◆ Throw the beanbag up in the air and clap a rhythm pattern with your hands—toss, clap, clap, and catch.
◆ Throw two beanbags up in the air, one in each hand, and catch the beanbags with the same hand.
◆ Throw one beanbag up in the air and catch it with the opposite hand—for example, catch the beanbag thrown with the right hand in the left hand, and catch the beanbag thrown with the left hand in the right hand.
◆ Throw the beanbag up in the air and try to touch it with your right or left foot.
◆ Throw the beanbag in rhythmic sequences that include left, right, and both hands; for example, left hand—toss and catch two times; both hands—toss and catch one time; and right hand—toss and catch two times; then repeat.
◆ Throw a beanbag up in the air and try to catch it with eyes closed. (This activity requires the child to visualize the path that the beanbag will follow in its descent and to predict where it will fall.)

Teacher Observations

Motor Planning: Does the child move his or her body to catch the beanbag?

Ocular Control: Does the child sustain visual fixation and tracking on the beanbag while catching it?

Beanbag Pass

Equipment

Large beanbags—one for each group of four to six children (see Appendix A)

Activity

The children sit or stand in a circle and pass a beanbag around in a specified manner. They can pass using both hands together or pass the beanbag from one hand to the other hand. Try passing overhead, through the legs, in back of the body, crossing hands, around the body, and so on.

For older children who may enjoy a more competitive game of *Beanbag Pass,* try *Relay Races* or *Hot Potato.*

Relay Races: Have the children form two lines and pass the desired number of beanbags in any designated manner.

Hot Potato: Have the children stand or sit in a circle and pass the beanbag in a hot potato–style around the circle while music plays. When the music stops, whoever is holding the beanbag must go to the center of the circle and jog or jump in place to the count of ten.

The weight of the beanbag can be varied for larger or smaller children.

Teacher Observations

Coordinating Body Sides: Is the child able to cross the midline of his or her body when passing the beanbag?

Motor Planning: Can the child pass a beanbag in the designated manner?

Beanbag Sequence

Equipment

Beanbags—one for each child
Weighted plastic pop bottles—one for each child (see Appendix A)
Start and throw lines, 12–15 feet apart—masking tape may be used

Activity

The children line up along the starting line. One beanbag for each child is placed on the throw line and a weighted plastic pop bottle is positioned 5 feet beyond each beanbag. The teacher chooses a sequence of motor actions for each child, such as hop on one foot twice, take a giant step, and jump one time. The child performs this sequence of motor actions as he or she moves toward the throw line. The child then picks up a beanbag, throws it at the bottle, and walks back to the start line. The teacher names one of the children to reposition the bottles and beanbags.

Teacher Observations

Auditory Processing: Does the child attend to and follow the directions?

Motor Planning: Can the child sequence the motor actions?

Beanbag Target

Equipment

Beanbags—one for each child
Weighted plastic pop bottle—one for each pair of two children (see Appendix A)
Parallel lines, 12–15 feet apart—masking tape may be used

Activity

The children divide into pairs and line up on the parallel lines, facing each other. A bottle is placed in the center between each pair of children. Each child is given a colored beanbag. As one or two colors are called, the children with those colors throw their beanbags in a designated manner, such as underhand, overhand, under the knee, through a bent elbow, and so on.

Teacher Observations

Body Awareness: Does the child attempt to control the thrust of his or her throw in order to hit the target?

Motor Planning: Can the child coordinate the position from which to throw the beanbag?

Visual-Spatial Perception: Is the child successful in correcting inaccurate throws?

Beanbags in a Basket

Equipment

Beanbags—one for each child
Containers or baskets of varying sizes

Activity

The children form a large circle around one or more containers. The children hold their beanbags and progress in a circle by walking, knee-walking, jumping, hopping, skipping, and so on, as instructed. Music or a song can be used to designate a period of time to circle a target. On command, the children stop. Each child takes a turn at throwing a beanbag in the basket, as directed; for example, the beanbags can be tossed underhand, overhand, under the leg, between the legs, over the shoulder, and so on. When all the beanbags have been thrown, one child is delegated to collect and redistribute them.

This activity can be made more challenging by varying the diameter of the container, the height of the container, or the distance the children stand from the container.

Teacher Observations

Auditory Processing: Can the child control the impulse to throw the beanbag until his or her name is called?

Body Awareness: Is the child able to adjust the intensity of his or her throwing to compensate for changes in distance?

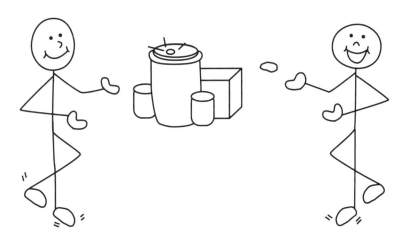

Toss Across

Equipment

Beanbags—one for each pair of children

Activity

Divide the class into two groups. The groups stand 10 to 15 feet apart, one group facing the other. Have the children take turns throwing a beanbag to their partner. If the partner does not catch the beanbag, he or she must take a step closer. The object of the game is to catch the beanbag each time so that the child does not have to move forward. This activity can be played in reverse, the child stepping back each time he or she catches the beanbag.

As the children become more familiar with the rules, more than one child at a time may throw. For example, all of the children with a specific-colored beanbag can throw simultaneously. This activity also can be varied by throwing while lying on the stomach, half-kneeling, kneeling, or squatting.

Teacher Observations

Body Awareness: Is the child able to control the force and distance of the throw?

Visual-Spatial Perception: Is the child successful at correcting inaccurate throws?

Toss at a Rolling Ball

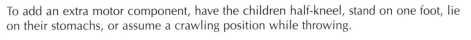

Equipment

Beanbags—one for each child
Playground ball
Parallel lines, 10–12 feet apart—masking tape or yarn may be used

Activity

The children are divided into two groups and seated facing each other on the parallel lines. One child is selected to help the teacher roll the ball between the two rows of children. Each child is given a beanbag to throw at the ball as it is rolled back and forth between the rows.

To add an extra motor component, have the children half-kneel, stand on one foot, lie on their stomachs, or assume a crawling position while throwing.

Teacher Observations

Motor Planning: Is the child able to time the throw to hit the ball when it passes?

Ocular Control: Can the child visually track the moving target?

Toss at a Target

Equipment

Beanbags of various sizes and weights
Targets: plastic bottles, plastic bowling pins, hula hoops, laundry baskets, boxes,
    wastebaskets, buckets, coffee cans, or lines made with masking tape

Activity

Beanbags can be thrown using a variety of throwing techniques, body postures, and
throwing styles. The distance of the line or target can be varied to change the motor
challenge.

Throw the beanbags over a line using a variety of throwing techniques, such as
overhand, underhand, with the right hand, with the left hand, or with both hands.

Throw the beanbags over a line using various body postures, such as kneeling, half-
kneeling, on hands and knees, and side-lying. In addition, vary the throwing techniques.

Throw the beanbags at or into a target using various throwing styles, such as over the
shoulder, under one leg, and between both legs.

Throw the beanbags at a target while going down a playground slide.

Teacher Observations

Body Awareness: Does the child adjust the force of the throw when the weight of the
beanbag or the distance from the target is changed?

Ocular Control: Does the child look at the target when throwing the beanbag?

Toss, Jump, Pick Up

Equipment

Large beanbags—one for each child
Start and finish lines, 12–15 feet apart—masking tape may be used (see Appendix A)

Activity

The children line up on the start line. As each name is called, the designated child tosses his or her beanbag forward. Without taking extra steps, the child then jumps over the beanbag, reaches down, picks it up, and throws it again to repeat the sequence. A child must start over if the beanbag is thrown too far to successfully jump over it, if extra steps are taken, or balance is lost. The children repeat this sequence until they reach the finish line.

Teacher Observations

Perception of Movement: Can the child jump and maintain foot placement without losing balance?

Visual-Spatial Perception: Can the child judge the approximate distance he or she can jump and then throw the beanbag the correct distance?

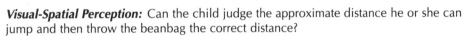

Turtle Races

Equipment

Turtle shells—large beanbags, jackets, blankets, or throw rugs
Start and finish lines, 12–15 feet apart—masking tape or yarn may be used

Activity

The children line up at the start line, forming teams for relays. Blankets, jackets, or rugs are placed on a child's back as a shell. The child crawls to the finish line, trying not to lose the shell.

To vary this activity, the children can place objects on their stomachs and crab-walk for a hermit crab race.

Teacher Observations

Body Awareness: Is the child able to maintain the posture necessary to keep from losing the item being balanced?

Perception of Touch: Does the child tolerate the texture or feel of the shell?

Games with Easily Made Equipment

Games with Easily Made Equipment

Primary Sensory and Motor Components Challenged in Each Activity

	AUDITORY PROCESSING	BODY AWARENESS	COORDINATING BODY SIDES	FINE MOTOR	MOTOR PLANNING	OCULAR CONTROL	ORAL MOTOR SKILLS	PERCEPTION OF MOVEMENT	PERCEPTION OF TOUCH	VISUAL-SPATIAL PERCEPTION
A-Tisket, A-Tasket	◆				◆					
Box Games			◆					◆		◆
Building Block Race Track		◆			◆					◆
Catch Ball in a Cup					◆	◆				
Catch with a Scoop		◆	◆		◆					
Circle Bunt Ball			◆		◆	◆		◆		
Cookie Baking			◆						◆	
Don't Spill the Cargo		◆						◆		
Dress-Up Relay				◆	◆				◆	
Feed the Elephant				◆						◆
Grab Bag	◆								◆	
Hopscotch					◆			◆		◆
Musical Chairs	◆				◆					
Pass It On									◆	◆
Pop Goes the Weasel			◆					◆		
Popcorn Popper	◆				◆		◆			

Continued on page 81

Games with Easily Made Equipment

Primary Sensory and Motor Components Challenged in Each Activity

Continued from page 80

	AUDITORY PROCESSING	BODY AWARENESS	COORDINATING BODY SIDES	FINE MOTOR	MOTOR PLANNING	OCULAR CONTROL	ORAL MOTOR SKILLS	PERCEPTION OF MOVEMENT	PERCEPTION OF TOUCH	VISUAL-SPATIAL PERCEPTION
Rhythm Sticks	◆		◆		◆					
Streamers			◆		◆					
Textured Finger Paints		◆							◆	
Who Stole the Cookie	◆		◆		◆					
Wiffle® Ball Catch					◆	◆				
Yarn Packages			◆		◆			◆	◆	

A-Tisket, A-Tasket

Equipment

Handkerchief, tissue, or beanbag

Activity

The children sit in a circle (use floor markers if needed). One child is chosen to be "It" and stands outside of the circle holding a handkerchief. As the children sing, "It" skips or animal-walks around the outside of the circle. During the words "I dropped it," "It" drops the handkerchief behind any child he or she chooses. "It" then continues around the circle in a hurry back to the empty space. The new child becomes "It," picks up the handkerchief, and tries to tag the child who dropped the handkerchief. Children can progress around the circle in opposite directions to avoid racing.

> ### Song
> A tisket, a tasket
> A green and yellow basket
> I wrote a letter to my love
> And on the way *I dropped it*
> *I dropped it, I dropped it*
> And on my way *I dropped it*
> A little boy (girl) picked it up
> And put it in his (her) pocket

This activity can be varied by having each child hold a bleach bottle scoop behind his or her back (see Appendix A). The child who is "It" drops a beanbag into the bleach bottle scoop of any child he or she chooses. The new child then progresses around the circle, carrying the beanbag in his or her scoop.

Teacher Observations

Auditory Processing: Does the child follow through with appropriate timing to the directions of the song?

Motor Planning: Can the child execute various patterns of movement? Can the child follow the correct sequence and direction of play?

Games With Easily Made Equipment

Box Games

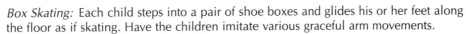

Equipment

Shoe boxes or cereal boxes, tissue boxes, or paper plates—two for each child

Activity

Box Skating: Each child steps into a pair of shoe boxes and glides his or her feet along the floor as if skating. Have the children imitate various graceful arm movements.

Box Water Skiing: Each child steps into a pair of shoe boxes and is pulled along by holding the ends of a jump rope that another child or adult pulls.

Box Train: Each child steps into a pair of shoe boxes and follows a designated path made with masking tape. Vary the path with straight and curved lines. Stuffed animals, books, or other objects can be held while following the "track," with pickup and delivery points along the way.

Box Gallop: Each child places one foot in a shoe box, leaving the other foot free. The children then gallop like horses. First, have the lead foot be the one in the box. Signal the time to alternate the lead foot by blowing a whistle, by stopping the music, or by clapping your hands.

Box Relay: The class is divided into two or more teams. Each team is given two shoe boxes to step into. The first person on each team races to a designated point and returns to his or her team, passing the boxes to the next person in line. The team to finish first is the winner. Try this game using only one box for each team, in a galloping motion.

Teacher Observations

Coordinating Body Sides: Can the child coordinate both feet alternately without falling?

Perception of Movement: Is the child able to maintain balance and postural stability while moving with his or her feet in the boxes?

Visual-Spatial Perception: Can the child stay on the designated path, especially as he or she moves around curves?

Building Block Race Track

Equipment

Cardboard boxes (a variety of sizes, 10–15 per class)
Wooden building blocks
Small cars, trucks, or trains
Chalk, masking tape, or hook and loop strips
Balance beam, if available

Activity

Cross Country: Draw a narrow road on the carpet in a large oval shape, using chalk, masking tape, or hook and loop strips. A balance beam can be set up along one of the roads. Begin by building a box structure on either side of one end of the road so that children can go under a bridge or through a tunnel. Each child takes a turn on the road in the designated manner, for example, crawling, knee walking, or heel-toe walking.

Encourage the students to take turns setting up and building a structure.

Car Races: The game can be played with wooden building blocks and small cars, trucks, or trains. The idea is to work on the ability to construct a specific structure. Set up the track and build a simple block structure for the car to go in, around, or through. Give the student a duplicate set of blocks to build the same structure. Have that student go around the track with a car while the other children cheer. Groups should be no larger than seven students so that each student will get a turn. It is an important part of this activity to have the other students watching as each child builds a structure so that they may learn construction strategies in the process.

Note: The boxes are usually good to have around for only a week or two. While you have them, remember they are fun to use for a variation of *Musical Chairs, Crab-Walk Soccer,* and various target games.

Teacher Observations

Body Awareness: Can the child maneuver his or her body around the course, making good adjustments in posture when balance is challenged?

Motor Planning: Is the child able to plan his or her body movements to stay on the track? Is the child able to duplicate and construct a meaningful or functional structure?

Visual-Spatial Perception: Is the child able to move within the boundaries of the track? Can the child stay on the track with his or her body or car?

Catch Ball in a Cup

Equipment

Ping-Pong or tennis ball—one for each child
Plastic cups—one for each child

Activity

The children stand arms-width apart in a line. Each child is given a cup for one hand and a ball for the other hand. The child bounces and catches the ball in the cup, as directed by the teacher. For example, "Everyone bounce the ball on the count of three and catch it."

To reduce distraction, children may take their turns when their name or number is called. Allow plenty of time for experimentation.

The motor demands of this activity can be increased by throwing and catching with a partner.

Teacher Observations

Motor Planning: Is the child able to time hand movements in order to catch the ball?

Ocular Control: Can the child maintain visual contact with the ball? Or does the child tend to focus on the cup?

Catch with a Scoop

Equipment

Beanbags—one for every two children
Bleach bottle scoops—one for every two children
Start and finish lines—masking tape or chalk may be used

Activity

The children pair off, one with a scoop on the start line, one with a beanbag on the finish line. Start and finish lines are approximately 10–15 feet apart. The child with the beanbag throws it to the child with the scoop. If the child catches the beanbag, he or she may take one step forward. The child with the scoop then tosses the beanbag. When the children meet, they exchange equipment and repeat the process, stepping back one step after each catch.

If there is a sufficient number of scoops, both children may use them; this is a more difficult task.

A timing sequence may be added. For example, have the children count to a designated number and then toss the beanbag. Also, the children can be cued to throw the beanbag by stopping and starting music.

Teacher Observations

Body Awareness: Does the child move arms and body to reach out to catch the beanbag?

Coordinating Body Sides: Is the child able to throw the beanbag using the scoop?

Motor Planning: Does the child maintain an upward tilt to the scoop so that the beanbag will not fall out?

Circle Bunt Ball

Equipment

Two-handed bottle bat—one for each child (see Appendix A)
Tennis ball

Activity

The children form a circle and lie on their stomachs facing each other. Each child holds the bat with two hands and bunts the ball across the circle. The object is to keep the ball rolling and inside the circle.

To avoid fatigue, allow the child to use one hand on the bat or change to a sitting or kneeling position. This activity also can work well in small groups or pairs.

Teacher Observations

Coordinating Body Sides: Can the child keep both hands on the bat to hit the ball, or does he or she try to let go with one hand?

Motor Planning: Can the child time his or her movements in order to make contact with the ball?

Ocular Control: Does the child follow the movement of the ball with his or her eyes?

Perception of Movement: Is the child able to hold his or her head and upper trunk up against gravity, thereby freeing the arms to use the bat?

Cookie Baking

Equipment

Two-handed bottle bat—one for every two children (see Appendix A)

Activity

Divide the children into pairs. One child becomes the "cookie dough" and lies flat on his or her stomach. The baker "rolls" out the dough, using the two-handed bat as a rolling pin. Roll each arm, leg, and back with firm pressure. When the rolling is finished, the baker can draw a shape on the back to decorate the cookie. The child who is the dough tries to guess what shape was drawn. The children then trade positions.

Some children may not tolerate having another child "roll" them but may accept this activity if they are able to "roll" themselves.

Teacher Observations

Coordinating Body Sides: Can the child smoothly roll the bat using both hands?

Perception of Touch: Does the child on the floor tolerate both the firm pressure of the rolling and the light pressure of a finger drawing on his or her back?

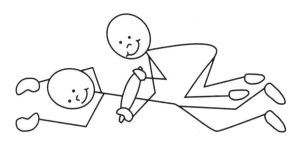

Don't Spill the Cargo

Equipment

Container: saucepan; tray; plastic cup, spoons, or measuring cups (one for each team)
Objects to be transported: cotton balls or lentils, popcorn, rice, water, eggs, candy-
  covered chocolates
Buckets, tubs, large bowls (one for each team)

Activity

Children are divided into groups of about four to six children, forming teams. From the
start line, a child transports a spillable object in a container to a container at the finish
line approximately 10–15 feet away. The object is relayed until each child has had a
turn. The class attempts to cooperate by successfully transporting as much of the object
as possible. Carefully measure the contents of each container after the relay.

The class works together to improve the amount transported and the time it takes for
them to finish. This can be a fun activity to work into a science or math class; graphs can
be drawn and material can be weighed.

Teacher Observations

Body Awareness: Is the child able to stabilize his or her body to carry a full container to
the finish line?

Perception of Movement: Does the child make appropriate body adjustments to avoid
tipping the container?

Dress-Up Relay

Equipment

Clothing: large shirts, coats, sweaters, pants, shorts, kneesocks, mittens
Two parallel lines—10–12 feet apart—made with masking tape or chalk

Activity

Children line up on the first line. The teacher puts an item of clothing on the second line, directly across from each child. The children are asked to knee-walk, hop, skip, jump, or animal-walk to their piece of clothing and put it on. After dressing, each child progresses in the designated manner back to the first line.

This activity can be varied by having pairs of children sit opposite each other on the line. Give each child an article of clothing to wear. Once they are dressed, the pairs progress to the center, exchange clothing, and return to their line. By eliminating buttons, cutting off sleeves, or using oversized clothing, this task can progress to various skill levels.

Teacher Observations

Fine Motor: Does the child have difficulty with fastening?

Motor Planning: Is the child able to put on the piece of clothing correctly?

Perception of Touch: Does the child object to various textures of clothing?

Feed the Elephant

Equipment

Cylinders made of rolled gray construction paper fastened with paper clips—one for each group of four children

Activity

Children wad paper into small balls to form peanuts. Place cylinder (the elephant's trunk) on its side or end. The children lie on their stomachs, trying to flip the paper peanut into the elephant's trunk.

To avoid fatigue, children may change position to hands and knees or to kneeling. To increase the difficulty of the game, vary the distance of the elephant's trunk from the child.

Teacher Observations

Fine Motor: Does the child have the dexterity to flip the paper peanut?

Visual-Spatial Perception: Can the child alter the force of the flip to improve target accuracy?

Grab Bag

Equipment

Paper or cloth bag—one for each child
Small common objects: spoon, spool of thread, penny, dice, bead, pencil, small ball, piece of fabric, feather, sponge, key, paper clip, leaf, rock, fruit

Activity

Fill the bags with common objects. Seat the children in a circle and give each one a bag. The teacher may give either verbal or visual instructions—the object can be described or held up for all to see. The students then use their hands without looking to find the designated objects in the bags.

Students are encouraged to manipulate the objects and feel for the corners, roundness, texture, and length. Some classes may need to see all of the objects before they are hidden in the bag. Have students take turns being the leader and have them try to describe what to look for.

Teacher Observations

Auditory Processing: Is the child able to find the object based on the verbal description?

Perception of Touch: Is the child able to find the common object by touch in a reasonable amount of time?

Hopscotch

Equipment

Chalk or tape

Lagger (for example, flat stone or beanbag)

Activity

Make a hopscotch court using chalk or tape, numbering each of the boxes. Four to six children can participate on each court; court formation can be varied to meet the skill level of the classroom. Each player has a lagger. The first player tosses his or her lagger into box number one. That player must hop over the box and land into the next box on either one foot or two feet without stepping on or over the line to the next box. The child continues on to the end.

The general rule is to hop on one foot in the single boxes and on two feet in the double boxes. In the last box the child jumps, making a half turn, and proceeds back to his or her lagger. The child then picks it up without falling and continues out of the court. The process is repeated until the lagger is thrown to the last box.

This activity may be modified to meet the individual child's skill level. Some children may need to jump with two feet instead of hopping or may perform better with a reduced number of boxes. Rules regarding stepping on the line may be eliminated. Children may be given several chances to set the lagger in the correct box.

Teacher Observations

Motor Planning: Is the child able to jump a different course each time the lagger is on a different square?

Perception of Movement: Can the child jump and maintain foot placement without losing his or her balance?

Visual-Spatial Perception: Can the child judge the approximate distance he or she can jump or throw to avoid touching the line?

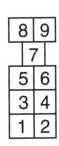
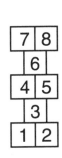
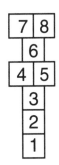

Musical Chairs

Equipment

Carpet squares, beanbags, or boxes—one for each child

Activity

The game is played using beanbags, carpet squares, or boxes in place of chairs. The children walk around the circle. The game is played much like the traditional musical chairs; however, no one is eliminated.

When the music stops, each child must stand on a beanbag, sit on a carpet square, or crawl into a box. The mode of movement may be varied each time; try knee-walking, walking backward, crawling, and animal-walking.

For older children, designate one beanbag, carpet square, or box, as the winner's spot. That person then chooses the next mode of movement.

Teacher Observations

Auditory Processing: Does the child respond quickly to musical cues? Does the child retain the concept of the game?

Motor Planning: Is the child able to perform the various modes of movement?

Pass It On

Equipment

Pencil
Paper

Activity

The children are divided into groups and seated train-style, facing one another's back. The last child in the line draws a letter, number, or shape on the person's back directly in front of him or her. The child who has the design drawn on his or her back then draws what he or she experiences on the back of the child in front of him or her. This is repeated until the first child in line receives the tactile message. This child then draws on paper or the chalkboard what was felt. The last child in line verifies the correctness of the message.

The order of the children may be rotated to facilitate the accuracy of the message.

To vary the level of difficulty, try rhythmical tapping on one another's back or using consecutive letters to convey simple words or messages.

Teacher Observations

Perception of Touch: Does the child complain of unusual tickling or pain when the message is drawn?

Visual-Spatial Perception: Is the child able to duplicate the design accurately?

Pop Goes the Weasel

Equipment

Weighted plastic pop bottles—one for every three children (see Appendix A)

Activity

The children sit in a circle, passing the bottles and singing *Pop! Goes the Weasel*. They must pass the bottles very quietly. When *Pop! Goes the Weasel* is sung, all those with bottles shake them. Bottles can be passed in a variety of ways—behind the back, overhead, under the legs, and so on.

Song:
All around the mulberry bush
The monkey chased the weasel
The weasel thought it all in fun
Pop! goes the weasel.

Teacher Observations

Coordinating Body Sides: Can the child easily cross the body's midline when passing the bottle?

Perception of Movement: Can the child control his or her movements so that the beans cannot be heard during the beginning of the song?

Popcorn Popper

Equipment

Weighted plastic pop bottles—one for every four children (see Appendix A)

Activity

The children sit in a circle. The weighted plastic pop bottle is passed around the circle in a designated manner. For example, the bottle can be passed with two hands, around the back, or overhead. The children chant *The Popcorn Popper Goes Pop!*

The object of the game is to pass the bottle very quietly until they hear the word "pop." Each time the word "pop" is sung, the children shake the bottle making a popping noise.

Chant
The popcorn popper goes POP!
The popcorn popper goes POP!
The popcorn popper goes POP, POP, POP!
The popcorn popper goes POP!

Teacher Observations

Auditory Processing: Is the child able to sequence the correct number of "pops"?

Motor Planning: Is the child able to pass the weighted plastic pop bottle in the designated manner?

Oral Motor Skills: Can the child say "pop" articulating the beginning and ending "P" sound?

Rhythm Sticks

Equipment

One set of rhythm sticks per child (see Appendix A)
Music: simple songs

Activity

Rhythm sticks, sometimes called lummi sticks, are used to tap to a rhythm of a familiar rhyme or song.

Variations include combinations of tapping sticks together. Try tapping a body part, tapping the floor, tapping the ends of the sticks, tapping high, tapping low, tapping to the right, tapping to the left, or tapping under a raised knee. Let your music suggest your movements.

Teacher Observations

Auditory Processing: Does the child tap at the correct auditory cue?

Coordinating Body Sides: Can the child simultaneously tap the sticks?

Motor Planning: Is the child able to sequence several combinations of tapping movements?

Streamers

Equipment

Streamers—two for each child (see Appendix A)

Activity

The children imitate the leader by forming circles, figure eights, letters, numbers, and so on, using whole-arm movements. This may be done to music once the children have had some practice.

A different color streamer for each hand may be useful in teaching left- versus right-hand discrimination.

Teacher Observations

Coordinating Body Sides: Can the child coordinate both hands together when performing mirror (same) movements and opposite movements? Does the child turn his or her whole body to avoid crossing the midline?

Motor Planning: Does the child need to watch his or her arms in order to execute motor patterns?

Textured Finger Paints

Equipment

Butcher or finger-painting paper

Finger paints

Textures: sand, seeds (poppy, sesame, celery, bird, sunflower), rice, uncooked hot cereals, lentils, fine macaroni

Tape

Newsprint

Activity

Cover the table top with butcher paper and secure the ends with tape. Give each child some finger paint and let the child choose a variety of textures. Once the child has made a design, a print can be made by pressing newsprint or other plain paper over it.

Seasonal pictures can be made by cutting shapes from the finger paint table to make pumpkins, ghosts, snowmen, bunnies, ducks, stars and stripes, and so on.

Try finger painting gently over macaroni, rice, lentils, and other materials that have been glued onto the paper.

Teacher Observations

Body Awareness: Is the child able to keep the paint confined to the appropriate space, or does he or she unknowingly get paint all over himself or herself?

Perception of Touch: Is the child uncomfortable getting his or her hands into the different textures?

Who Stole the Cookie

Equipment

Blank cards—one for each child

Activity

The children sit on the floor in a circle. Give each child a card face down. One of the cards has previously been designated as the cookie. While children chant, they keep beat by clapping, tapping, or using other rhythmical body movements.

Group: "Who stole the cookie from the cookie jar?" "(Name of child) stole the cookie from the cookie jar."

Child: "Who, me?"

Group: "Yes, you!"

(Child named turns over his or her card and responds)

Child: "Not me," or "Yes, me."

Group: "Then who?"

If the child named did not have the cookie, then he or she chooses the next child and the sequence is repeated.

This game can be integrated into a reading or math lesson. Each child is given a card with a different spelling word or math problem. The teacher designates one card as the cookie. When a child's name is called, the child turns over his or her card and spells the word or solves the problem to see if he or she has the cookie.

Teacher Observations

Auditory Processing: Can the child remember the chant and respond accordingly?

Coordinating Body Sides: Does the child have difficulty establishing or maintaining the rhythm?

Motor Planning: Is the child able to imitate and sequence the movement patterns, for example, the hand clapping and the chanting?

Wiffle® Ball Catch

Equipment

Wiffle® ball catcher—one for each child (see Appendix A)
Wiffle® ball attached to a bleach bottle

Activity

Have the child try to catch the ball in the Wiffle® ball scoop. See how many times the child can catch the ball without missing. Try catching on the count of three—"one, two, three, catch!"

Teacher Observations

Motor Planning: Does the child have difficulty timing the catch?

Ocular Control: Does the child keep his or her eye on the ball?

Yarn Packages

Equipment

Thick yarn, 12–15-foot lengths—one for every two children
Craft sticks—one for every two children
Tape

Activity

Have the children tape one end of the yarn to the stick and wrap the yarn around it. Children pair off and take turns wrapping the yarn around each other between the shoulders and knees. When the "package" has been wrapped, the child turns his or her body to unwrap. As he or she turns, the child with the stick quickly winds the yarn back onto the stick. The children then change places.

For a variation, the child who is wrapped with yarn stands still while the other child unwraps the "package." Mummies also can be made using toilet paper.

If the child finds it too stressful to have the yarn around the arms, then keep the arms free.

Teacher Observations

Coordinating Body Sides: Can the child perform the bilateral task of wrapping the yarn around the stick?

Motor Planning: Can the child figure out which direction to turn his or her body in order to wind or unwind the yarn?

Perception of Movement: Does the child easily become dizzy during this activity? Does the child continue to spin after he or she is unwrapped? Can the child maintain balance while turning?

Perception of Touch: Does the child react negatively to the sensation of the yarn?

Traditional Children's Games

Traditional Children's Games

Primary Sensory and Motor Components Challenged in Each Activity

	AUDITORY PROCESSING	BODY AWARENESS	COORDINATING BODY SIDES	FINE MOTOR	MOTOR PLANNING	OCULAR CONTROL	ORAL MOTOR SKILLS	PERCEPTION OF MOVEMENT	PERCEPTION OF TOUCH	VISUAL-SPATIAL PERCEPTION
Aerobic Stepping	◆	◆	◆		◆					
Animal-Walks		◆			◆					
Charades		◆			◆					
Duck, Duck, Goose	◆				◆				◆	
Hand Clapping			◆		◆					
Hokey Pokey	◆	◆						◆		
Johnny Pounds with One Hammer			◆		◆					
Lion Hunt		◆			◆					
London Bridge					◆			◆	◆	
Melt the Ice		◆			◆					
Mirror Image		◆			◆	◆				
Pretzel		◆			◆					
Progressive Aerobics	◆		◆		◆			◆		
Red Light, Green Light	◆	◆			◆					
Red Rover					◆			◆		
Ring Around the Rosy	◆	◆						◆		
Spinning Statue Freeze		◆			◆			◆		
The Thousand-Legged Worm	◆	◆			◆			◆		
The Tortoise and the Hare	◆				◆					
We Waded in the Water		◆							◆	

Aerobic Stepping

Equipment

None

Activity

The children continuously march in place or in a circle while performing the activities listed and chanting to the tune of *Step in Time* (Sherman, R. M., 1964). With each round, change the activity slightly. For example:

Chant
Kick your knees up
Swing your arms
Close your eyes
Step so soft (hard, fast, slow)
Circle your arms
Touch your shoulders
Clap your hands
Kick your right leg

Teacher Observations

Auditory Processing: Can the child process the words to the song and execute the correct movement?

Body Awareness: Can the child move his or her limbs without looking at his or her movements?

Coordinating Body Sides: Does the child maintain a reciprocal stepping pattern, that is, step with the right foot and then the left foot?

Motor Planning: Does the child have difficulty stepping and doing arm and finger movements simultaneously?

Animal-Walks

Equipment

None

Activity

Animal-walks can be practiced to music, used in place of running or walking in traditional children's games, or used in relay races.

Teacher Observations

Body Awareness: Can the child make the postural adjustments necessary to assume and maintain the various positions?

Motor Planning: Can the child copy the designated animal-walk without physical cues?

Bear

Assume a creeping posture, progress forward and back, moving the arms and legs of one side simultaneously; keep the head down.

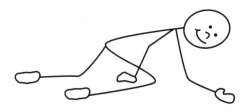

Bird

Stand on tiptoes and wave the arms slowly up and down. As the "wings" move faster, run on tiptoe around as if flying. As the flapping slows down, the bird slowly comes to a stop.

Continued on page 109

Animal-Walks

Continued from page 108

Bunny

Squat low on heels and place the hands palm-down on the floor. Move the hands forward, then bring the feet forward between the hands with a little jump.

Crab

Squat, reach backward with the arms, and put both hands flat on the floor. Raise up until the head, neck, and body are in a straight line, then walk or run in this position.

Duck

Bend the knees and place the hands around the ankles. Walk forward one foot at a time, keeping the knees bent.

Continued on page 110

Animal-Walks

Continued from page 109

Elephant

Bend forward at the hips, allowing the arms to hang limp. Take big, lumbering steps while swaying from side to side, imitating an elephant and its trunk.

Inchworm

Support the body with hands and toes and keep the body in a straight line. With the hands remaining in place, walk toward the hands, taking tiny steps; keep the legs straight. Then, keeping the feet in place, walk the hands forward in tiny steps.

Horses Galloping

Gallop forward with the hands held as if holding reins. Change and lead off with opposite foot.

Continued on page 111

Animal-Walks

Continued from page 110

Horses Prancing

Stand straight, with the hands held as if holding reins. Lift one knee high with toes pointed. Just as the foot touches the ground again, lift the other knee vigorously. Repeat the steps in a rhythmic motion, with forward momentum.

Kangaroo

Stand with the feet together and bend the elbows out from the body. Let the hands dangle. Bend the knees and jump forward.

Monkey

With both hands on the floor, run forward, with the knees slightly bent.

Continued on page 112

Animal-Walks

Continued from page 111

Mule Kick

Squat and place the palms of the hands on the floor, between the knees. Bear weight on the hands and vigorously kick the feet backward. When the feet hit the ground, stand and take two steps forward. Repeat the sequence.

Rooster

Bend forward at the waist and grasp the ankles. Keep the knees straight and walk forward.

Seal

Lie face down on the floor and push the body up with extended arms. Walk forward with the arms while the feet drag behind.

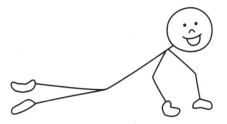

Charades

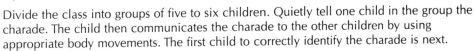

Equipment

None

Activity

Divide the class into groups of five to six children. Quietly tell one child in the group the charade. The child then communicates the charade to the other children by using appropriate body movements. The first child to correctly identify the charade is next.

Charades can be played using a number of different themes. It can be structured from a simple one-step sequence to a more complex sequence of actions. Pictures or written cue cards may be used for variation.

Suggested Themes

Animals: Elephant, donkey, rabbit, monkey

Emotions: Angry, happy, embarrassed, confused, frightened, surprised

Sports: Ice skating, skiing, soccer, hopscotch, roller skating, tennis, jump rope, archery

Familiar Tasks: Brushing hair/teeth, getting dressed, making a bed, washing dishes, emptying the trash

Occupations: Fire fighter, police officer, nurse, secretary

Teacher Observations

Body Awareness: Are the children able to coordinate their arms and legs in miming the charade? Does the child seem to lack awareness of what the body parts are doing?

Motor Planning: Is the child able to gesture appropriately when communicating the charade? How complex are the child's ideas for gesturing? Does the child use a single movement or a sequence of movements to describe the charade?

Duck, Duck, Goose

Equipment

None

Activity

The children sit in a circle or assume a designated posture. Carpet squares or place markers may be used for each child, if needed. One child is "It," and progresses around the outside of the circle in a designated animal-walk. As he or she passes each child, "It" taps the child gently, saying "duck" or "goose." If the child says "goose," then the child tapped pursues the child who is "It" around the circle in the same designated manner until the vacant space is reached. The child tapped then becomes "It" and repeats the process.

If the class becomes too chaotic during the chase sequence, have the child who is tapped move in the opposite direction to reach the empty space.

Hoppity-hop may be used for the older children.

Teacher Observations

Auditory Processing: Does the seated child anticipate and respond to the verbal cue of "goose"?

Motor Planning: Can the child copy the designated animal-walk without physical cues?

Perception of Touch: Does the seated child appear unaware of being touched or oversensitive to being touched when he or she is tapped?

Hand Clapping

The following clapping patterns are presented in a developmental sequence beginning with individual clapping patterns and progressing to clapping patterns with partners. They work well with almost any song and the timing can be altered to fit a particular rhythm. The simplest form of clapping is to repeat the same one-step pattern without crossing the midline of the body. Next in order of difficulty is to vary the clapping sequence, maintaining the same rhythm again without crossing the midline. Variations include assuming different body positions and clapping different body parts. Clapping variations that include crossing the body's midline are the most difficult and are presented last.

One-Step Clapping Pattern

◆ Clap own hands to music or rhymes

◆ Slap own thighs (knees, shoulders, elbow)

Two-Step Sequence

◆ Clap own hands; slap own thighs

◆ Clap own hands; tap own shoulders

◆ Clap own hands; tap own head

Continued on page 116

Hand Clapping

Continued from page 115

Two-Step Sequence with Repetitive Action

◆ Clap own hands twice; slap thighs twice

◆ Clap own hands three times; slap thighs three times

Three-Step Sequence

◆ Clap own hands once, slap thighs once, slap the floor once

◆ Clap own hands, slap backs of hands on thighs, slap the floor

Right and Left Hands Take Turns

◆ Clap, slap left hand on left thigh; clap, slap right hand on right thigh

◆ Clap, slap left hand on left thigh, slap right hand on right thigh; clap

Crossing the Midline of the Body

◆ Clap, cross arms and slap thigh

◆ Clap, slap left hand on right thigh, slap right hand on left thigh; clap

Partner Hand Clapping

◆ Clap own hands; slap partner's hands once

◆ Clap own hands twice; slap partner's hands twice

◆ Clap own hands once; slap partner's hands; slap own thighs

Continued on page 117

Hand Clapping

Continued from page 116

◆ Clap; slap partner's left hand with own right hand; slap partner's right hand with own left hand

◆ Clap; slap partner's right hand with own right hand; slap partner's left hand with own left hand

Teacher Observations

Coordinating Body Sides: Is the student able to cross his or her midline when clapping with a partner? Can both hands work together fluidly and with rhythm?

Motor Planning: Can the child duplicate a three-part sequence and repeat it rhythmically a number of times?

Hand Clapping Rhymes

A Sailor Went to Sea

A sailor went to sea, sea, sea,
To see what he could see, see
But all that he could see, see
Was the bottom of the deep blue sea, sea, sea.

Bingo

There was a farmer had a dog,
And BINGO was his name-O,
B-I-N-G-O
B-I-N-G-O
B-I-N-G-O
And BINGO was his name-O.

Down by the Banks

Down by the banks of the Hanky Panky,
Where the bullfrogs jump from bank to banky,
With an eeps, opps, oops, ups,
He missed the lily and he went ker-plop.

Hambone

Hambone, Hambone, have you heard?
Papa's gonna buy me a mockingbird.

If that mockingbird don't sing,
Papa's gonna buy me a diamond ring.

If that diamond ring don't shine,
Papa's gonna buy me a fishing line.

Hambone, Hambone, where you been?
Around the world and I'm going again.

Hambone, Hambone, where's your wife?
In the kitchen cooking rice.

Continued on page 119

Traditional Children's Games

Hand Clapping Rhymes

Continued from page 118

Head and Shoulders

Head and shoulders, Baby
One, two, three.
Head and shoulders, Baby
One, two, three.
Head and shoulders,
Head and shoulders,
Head and shoulders, Baby
One, two, three.

Knees and ankles, Baby
One, two, three.
Knees and ankles, Baby
One, two, three.
Knees and ankles,
Knees and ankles,
Knees and ankles, Baby
One, two, three.

Turn around, Baby

Touch the ground, Baby.

Head and Shoulders, Knees and Toes

Head and shoulders, knees and toes,
Knees and toes,
Head and shoulders, knees and toes,
Knees and toe-oe-oe-oes.
Eyes and ears and mouth and nose.
Head and shoulders, knees and toes,
Knees and toes.

Long Legged Sailor

Have you ev-er, ev-er, ev-er, in your long leg-ged life,
Seen a long leg-ged sai-lor and his long leg-ged wife?

No I've never, never, never in my long leg-ged life,
Seen a long leg-ged sailor and his long leg-ged wife.

Continued on page 120

Hand Clapping Rhymes

Continued from page 119

Miss Lucy Had a Baby

Miss Lucy had a baby,
She named him Tiny Tim.
She put him in the bathtub
To see if he could swim.

He drank up all the water.
He ate up all the soap.
He tried to eat the bathtub,
But it wouldn't go down his throat.

Miss Lucy called the doctor.
Miss Lucy called the nurse.
Miss Lucy called the lady
With the alligator purse.

Miss Mary Mack

Miss Mary Mack, Mack, Mack
All dressed in black, black, black
With silver buttons, buttons, buttons
All down her back, back, back.

She asked her mother, mother, mother
For fifteen cents, cents, cents
To see the elephant, elephant, elephant
Jump over the fence, fence, fence.

He jumped so high, high, high
He reached the sky, sky, sky
And didn't come back, back, back
Till the Fourth of July, ly, ly.

Peas Porridge Hot

Peas porridge hot
Peas porridge cold
Peas porridge in the pot
Nine days old.

Some like it hot
Some like it cold
Some like it in the pot
Nine days old.

Daddy likes it hot
Mommy likes it cold
I like it in the pot
Nine days old.

Continued on page 121

Hand Clapping Rhymes

Continued from page 120

Playmate

Playmate
Come out and play with me
And bring your dol-lies three
Climb up my ap-ple tree
Look down my rain barrel
Slide down my cel-lar door
And we'll be jol-ly friends
For ev-er more, more, more!

Pretty Little Dutch Girl

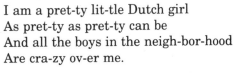

I am a pret-ty lit-tle Dutch girl
As pret-ty as pret-ty can be
And all the boys in the neigh-bor-hood
Are cra-zy ov-er me.

My boyfriend's name is Mellow
He comes from the land of Jello
With pickles for his toes
And a cherry for his nose
And that's the way my story goes.

Skida Marink

Skida Marink a-dink a-dink
Skida a-dink a-do.
I love you.

I love you in the morning,
And in the afternoon.
I love you in the evening,
And underneath the moon.

Oh skida marink a-dink a-dink,
Skida a-dink a-do.
I LOVE YOU.
I LOVE YOU!

Continued on page 122

Hand Clapping Rhymes

Continued from page 121

Ten Little Indians

One little, two little, three little Indians,
Four little, five little, six little Indians,
Seven little, eight little, nine little Indians,
Ten little Indian boys.

Ten little, nine little, eight little Indians,
Seven little, six little, five little Indians,
Four little, three little, two little Indians,
One little Indian boy.

The Bear Went Over the Mountain

The bear went over the mountain,
The bear went over the mountain,
The bear went over the mountain
To see what he could see.
And all that he could see,
And all that he could see
Was the other side of the mountain
Was all that he could see!

The bear went over the river,
The bear went over the river,
The bear went over the river
To see what he could see.
And all that he could see,
And all that he could see
Was the other side of the river,
The other side of the river,
The other side of the river
Was all that he could see!

Continued on page 123

Hand Clapping Rhymes

Continued from page 122

This Old Man

This old man he played ONE
He played knick-knack on his thumb
With a knick-knack patty wack
Give your dog a bone
This old man came rolling home.

This old man he played TWO
He played knick-knack on his shoe
With a knick-knack patty wack
Give your dog a bone
This old man came rolling home.

This old man he played THREE
He played knick-knack on his knee.

This old man he played FOUR
He played knick-knack on his door.

This old man he played FIVE
He played knick-knack on his hive.

This old man he played SIX
He played knick-knack on his sticks.

This old man he played SEVEN
He played knick-knack on his heaven.

This old man he played EIGHT
He played knick-knack on his gate.

This old man he played NINE
He played knick-knack on his time.

This old man he played TEN
He played knick-knack once again.

Hokey Pokey

Equipment

None

Activity

The children form a circle and follow the words of the song.

Stress only one body side throughout the activity to reinforce the concept of left or right. Vary the activity by performing it in standing, sitting, kneeling, and half-kneeling positions.

Song
You put your right hand in
You put your right hand out
You put your right hand in
And shake it all about.
You do the hokey-pokey
(bend elbows, wiggle fingers up, sway hips)
And you turn yourself around.
That's what it's all about!
(clap in rhythm)

Verses
◆ You put your right foot in . . .
◆ You put your right shoulder in . . .
◆ You put your right hip in . . .
◆ You put your head in . . .
◆ You put your whole self in . . .

Teacher Observations

Auditory Processing: Can the child imitate the words of the song?

Body Awareness: Can the child isolate the appropriate body part to move?

Perception of Movement: Can the child maintain orientation and place while turning? Can the child balance on one foot?

Johnny Pounds with One Hammer

Equipment

None

Activity

The children sit on the floor in a line and duplicate the rhythm and motions of the leader. The leader sings:

Song
Johnny pounds with one hammer,
One hammer, one hammer.
Johnny pounds with one hammer,
Now he pounds with two.
(Now he pounds with three.)

The leader pounds the floor with a fist. With each increase in number (one, two, three . . .), another part of the body is moved in unison to the beat. This continues until three or four body parts are "pounded" simultaneously. The tune ends with:

Johnny pounds with four hammers,
Now he is all through.

Keep this activity short because it can be fatiguing.

Teacher Observations

Coordinating Body Sides: Can the child maintain the rhythm of the activity? Can the child continue to maintain the rhythm as additional body parts assume the motion of the rhythm?

Motor Planning: Can the child direct his or her body to follow the leader?

Lion Hunt

Equipment

None

Activity

The children mime movements as the teacher narrates the actions involved in catching a lion while on a safari. Begin the game by clapping in rhythm to the chant.

Chant

Going on a lion hunt. (Clapping)
Going to catch a big one. (Clapping)
STOP. (Stop)

I see a dark, marshy jungle! (Hand over brow to imitate looking ahead.)
Can't go over.
Can't go under.
Let's go through. (Act out walking through a jungle.)

Repeat
Going on a lion hunt. (Clapping)
Going to catch a big one. (Clapping)
STOP. (Stop)

I see . . .

Continued on page 127

Lion Hunt

Continued from page 126

Include climbing in and out of a jeep, marching across hot sand (walk on tiptoes, on heels), climbing up and down a rope, walking through mud, swimming across a river, digging a trap, and paddling a canoe. On seeing the imaginary lion, the children freeze in a crouched position.

Children escape the lion by backtracking the sequence of actions. If space is limited, children can go through the actions standing in one place.

All ages can enjoy this. For older children, let them take turns narrating the story, or let some of them guess what is happening as other children perform the actions.

Teacher Observations

Body Awareness: Can the child maintain the postures with only verbal cues, or does the child need to copy the teacher or other children?

Motor Planning: Can the child easily mimic the postures?

London Bridge

Equipment

None

Activity

The children are divided into two groups. One group divides into pairs to form bridges, and the other group forms a line that will pass under the bridges. The children who form the bridges can do so by standing, kneeling, or half-kneeling and holding hands or sitting and joining feet. The children who pass under the bridge can walk, knee-walk, animal-walk, hop, skip, or jump.

Song
London Bridge is falling down,
Falling down, falling down.
London Bridge is falling down
My fair lady.

Verses
◆ Take the key and lock her up . . .
◆ Build it up with iron bars . . .
◆ Iron bars will bend and break . . .
◆ Build it up with silver and gold . . .

Teacher Observations

Motor Planning: Can the child adapt his or her movements to accommodate various size bridges?

Perception of Movement: Does the child have enough postural control to maintain position?

Perception of Touch: Does the child avoid or overreact to the physical contact involved in this game?

Melt the Ice

Equipment

None

Activity

Each child sits on the floor with knees bent and arms holding the knees closely to the chest. The teacher says, "Hug your knees as tightly as you can. Pretend you are an ice cube. The ice is slowly melting. You are melting into a nice, big puddle on the floor."

Slowly, each body part relaxes onto the floor.

A darkened room promotes a more relaxed atmosphere with less distraction. This activity is especially helpful at the end of a motor session when children seem to be overactive and need to be calmed down for academics.

Teacher Observations

Body Awareness: Can the child stiffen all of the body at one time to be an effective ice cube?

Motor Planning: Can the child relax just the one part of the body that is melting?

Mirror Image

Equipment

None

Activity

The children pair off, facing one another. The teacher instructs the children to pretend that they are looking in a mirror. One child of each pair is designated the mirror. When the child who is not the mirror moves, the one who is the mirror must move in the same manner. Initially, it will help the children to learn the activity if the child doing the action does it in slow motion. The teacher may designate the activity if the children have difficulty getting started.

With small groups, the teacher may wish to have only one person doing the action and all the others mirroring it. This variation enables the teacher to observe subtleties in performance.

To encourage the children to be more precise in their mirroring, teams can be organized to perform and to judge accuracy of movement.

Teacher Observations

Body Awareness: Can the child maintain body postures without looking at his or her own body?

Motor Planning: Does the child mirror the action or attempt to reverse it?

Ocular Control: Is the child able to sustain visual contact in order to duplicate all of the action?

Pretzel

Equipment

None

Activity

The children sit or stand in a line or a circle. They begin by pantomiming making pretzel dough. Next, they rub the dough all over themselves. Each child takes a turn being the "baker" and assumes a pretzel posture that all the others must imitate. The pretzel posture is chosen by the child. The posture may vary from a straight position to the arms crossing.

The children "bake" for 20 seconds by holding still. After this, the teacher and the "baker" test the children for "doneness" by gently pushing and pulling them. When testing for "doneness," give verbal cues such as "Make your arms very stiff so I can't move them," or "Let's see if I can bend this pretzel." If any part moves, they must "bake" a little longer. When all are "done," the next child takes a turn at assuming a new posture.

Teacher Observations

Body Awareness: Can the child hold a stationary posture?

Motor Planning: Can the child mimic postures or think up novel ones?

Progressive Aerobics

Equipment

None

Activity

This game is similar to the game *I Packed My Grandmother's Suitcase.*

The children stand in a circle. A designated child begins by saying, "I went to exercise class and I did *jumping jacks*" (exercise of child's choice). All the children in the circle demonstrate the action. The next child in the circle repeats the first action, saying, "I went to exercise class and I did *jumping jacks* and *push-ups*" (demonstrating choice of exercise). All the children do the movements as each exercise is named. This sequence continues until all the children have had a turn to add to the list of exercises. During their turn, encourage the children to remember the preceding exercises before adding one of their own.

Teacher Observations

Auditory Processing: Can the child remember the sequence of exercises that preceded his or her turn?

Coordinating Body Sides: Can the child smoothly execute bilateral exercises, such as jumping jacks or alternating toe touches?

Motor Planning: Do the movements resemble that of the stated exercise?

Perception of Movement: Can the child maintain balance and postural control for the various exercises?

Red Light, Green Light

Equipment

None

Activity

The children line up along the start line. If needed, start and finish lines may be made of masking tape or yarn. A leader stands at the finish line. Children progress according to a designated animal-walk whenever the leader says "green light." If a child fails to stop when "red light" is called, then he or she must return to the start line. If a child does not do the animal-walk in the manner designated, then he or she must return to the start line. When a child reaches the finish line, then he or she must progress backward toward the start line, again doing the designated animal-walk.

Stop-and-go signs or color cards may be used. Start by giving children both an auditory and visual cue; then see if they can attend to just a visual cue.

Teacher Observations

Auditory Processing: Can the child control the impulse to move until he or she hears the appropriate verbal cue?

Body Awareness: Can the child stop on "red light"?

Motor Planning: Can the child quickly and smoothly assume various animal-walk positions?

Red Rover

Equipment

None

Activity

The children are divided into two groups and lined up facing each other. Parallel start and finish lines, approximately 15 feet apart, made of masking tape or yarn, and a designated carpet square for each child to sit on may be used, if needed. The game is played much like the traditional *Red Rover;* however, a specific movement pattern (variations of rolling, crawling, wheelbarrow-walking, knee-walking, animal-walking, jumping, hopping, skipping) is called. For example, one team calls a child from the opposite team over: "Red Rover, Red Rover, send Cathy right over." This child moves in the designated manner over the line and sits with the new team. Cathy's team then calls another child over until every child has had a turn.

Teacher Observations

Motor Planning: Does the child smoothly execute the pattern of movement he or she has been given?

Perception of Movement: Can the child maintain balance and move in a straight line while rolling, hopping, and so on?

Ring Around the Rosy

Equipment

None

Activity

The children hold hands and walk around in a circle as they chant.

Chant
Ring-around-the-rosy
Pocket full of poseys
Ashes, ashes
All fall down.

Verses
◆ All clap hands
◆ All hop around
◆ All squat
◆ All jump up and down
◆ All turn half-way around

The children follow the action suggested in the last portion of each verse.

Having the children hold hands and face outward from the circle is more challenging than facing the center. To add a creative component to this activity, have each child name an alternate action.

Teacher Observations

Auditory Processing: Does the child follow the directions of the song?

Body Awareness: Is the child able to hold hands without dropping or squeezing the other child's hand?

Perception of Movement: Is the child able to balance while performing all of the motor actions, without dragging another child down?

Spinning Statue Freeze

Equipment

None

Activity

The children pair off, then grasp hands and spin around in a safe manner. It is usually best to have only one pair moving at a time. At the count of "1-2-3," they stop and assume a specific posture.

Suggested Postures

Animals: Elephant, donkey, rabbit, monkey

Emotions: Angry, happy, embarrassed, confused, frightened, surprised

Reflections: The child copies the partner's or teacher's position.

Robots: The child holds the posture. The teacher "activates the robot" by "turning on" one arm or leg at a time. The child maintains this action until every child has been "activated."

Teacher Observations

Body Awareness: Can the child make the body adjustments necessary to assume the posture with ease and maintain the position?

Motor Planning: Can the child copy another person's posture?

Perception of Movement: Does the child overly seek or avoid spinning? This activity may not be appropriate for children who seem to get out of control by spinning.

The Thousand-Legged Worm

Equipment

None

Activity

The children sit or assume the "all-fours" position (on hands and knees). Space the children so that everyone can see the leader. The children sing *The Thousand-Legged Worm* to the tune *Polly-Wolly Doodle* as they copy the leader in moving specific body parts.

Song
Oh, the thousand-legged worm
Oh, the thousand-legged worm
Oh, the thousand-legged worm
His head can turn.
(Leader turns head from side to side.)

Repeat the song and substitute body parts:

Verses
- His elbow can squirm
- His fingers can squirm
- His feet can turn
- His tongue can squirm
- His legs can turn

The children may stomp their feet to keep the rhythm.

Teacher Observations

Auditory Processing: Is the child able to respond to auditory cues for following directions or does he or she depend on visual cues only?

Body Awareness: Does the child tend to tire easily while maintaining the all-fours posture?

Motor Planning: Can the child imitate the movements of the leader?

Perception of Movement: When in the all-fours position, can the child maintain balance and posture while moving an arm or leg?

The Tortoise and the Hare

Equipment

None

Activity

Space the children at arm's length distance from one another. If needed, floor markers can be used to maintain spacing. The main goal is to keep the children moving in place to increase overall endurance. The teacher tells the story of the tortoise and the hare. When speaking about the tortoise, the children must step in slow motion. When speaking about the hare, the children step quickly.

Storyline: The hare makes fun of the slow, clumsy tortoise. The tortoise then challenges the hare to a footrace. The confident hare accepts the challenge. At the start of the race, the hare sprints out of sight, leaving the tortoise to plod along. The hare gets tired from the fast pace and stops to rest. But the tortoise keeps plodding along. (Repeat the sprinting and plodding sequence several times.) The hare falls asleep thinking he has the race almost won. The tortoise wins because he keeps pacing himself and doesn't stop and get distracted from his goal of making it to the finish line.

When the children are comfortable with this, add interesting dilemmas to the story, which require other movements; for example, run with hands over head, on hips, on shoulders, across shoulders, waving, and so on. The teacher can use instruments to maintain the tempo.

This activity is especially good on rainy days. Keep the activity short, about 3 to 6 minutes. This activity can be calming or stimulating, depending on the type of movements or storyline.

Teacher Observations

Auditory Processing: Does the child change the pace as the storyline varies?

Motor Planning: Can the child make appropriate changes in the tempo and in body positions?

We Waded in the Water

Equipment

None

Activity

The children sit or stand in a circle and, to the tune of *The Battle Hymn of the Republic*, sing:

Song

We waded in the water, and we got our feet all wet
We waded in the water, and we got our feet all wet
We waded in the water, and we got our feet all wet
But we didn't get our (clap, clap) wet (clap), yet (clap).

Repeat verses adding the next level of anatomy: ankles, knees, thighs, elbows, hands, etc. The children pat body parts when they are mentioned in the song.

Last Verse

We waded in the water and we finally got it wet . . .
We finally got our (clap) bathing suit (clap) wet.

This activity can be varied by using crepe paper streamers as the water. Some of the children wave them horizontally while other children stand in their path.

Teacher Observations

Body Awareness: Is the child able to identify body parts?

Perception of Touch: Does the child complain about or avoid this activity? Does the child rub his or her arms and legs excessively after the initial tactile input?

Jump Rope Games

Jump Rope Games

Primary Sensory and Motor Components Challenged in Each Activity

	AUDITORY PROCESSING	BODY AWARENESS	COORDINATING BODY SIDES	FINE MOTOR	MOTOR PLANNING	OCULAR CONTROL	ORAL MOTOR SKILLS	PERCEPTION OF MOVEMENT	PERCEPTION OF TOUCH	VISUAL-SPATIAL PERCEPTION
Pre-Jump Rope Games										
High Water-Low Water			◆		◆			◆		
Stationary Rope			◆		◆			◆		
Ocean Waves					◆					◆
Snake					◆					◆
Tug Boat		◆						◆		
Beginning Jump Rope Games										
Inside Outside					◆			◆		
Jump the Shot					◆	◆		◆		
Lasso Jump	◆				◆					
Jump Rope Games										
Blue Bells					◆			◆		
Easy Overhead					◆			◆		
Eskimo Jump Rope					◆					◆
Individual Jump Rope			◆		◆					
Advanced Jump Rope Games										
Cooperative Jump Rope					◆					◆
Egg Beater					◆					◆
Multiple Jump Rope					◆	◆				
Stunt Jump	◆		◆							

Pre-Jump Rope Games

Equipment

Jump rope, 12–15 feet long—one for every group of four to six children

Activities

High Water-Low Water

The rope is held in a stationary position by two people standing at each end. (Be sure that the rope is held loosely in the hands.) Each child attempts to jump over the rope. Alter the rope's height; try it limbo style.

Stationary Rope

Stretch out the rope in a straight line on the ground. The children start at one end of the rope and jump from side to side over the rope to the other end. Have them try to jump forward and backward over the rope and continue down to the end.

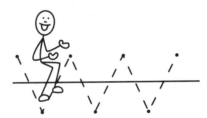
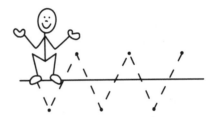

Teacher Observations

Coordinating Body Sides: Is the child able to jump with both feet at the same time?

Motor Planning: Is the child able to jump backward and sideways as well as forward?

Perception of Movement: Does the child lose balance when jumping over the rope?

Pre-Jump Rope Games

Equipment

Jump rope, 12–15 feet long—one for each group of four to six children

Activities

Ocean Waves

Two rope turners make waves in a rope by moving their arms up and down. The children should try to time it so as to jump over a low part of the wave.

Snake

Two rope turners move the rope back and forth to make a snake motion. The height and width of the moving snake can be altered.

Teacher Observations

Motor Planning: Does the child time the jump to coincide with the rope's position?

Visual-Spatial Perception: Does the child appear to perceive the correct height of the rope and jump accordingly?

Pre-Jump Rope Games

Equipment

Jump rope, 12–15 feet long—one for every group of two to four children

Activity

Tug Boat

A pair of children sit, kneel, half-kneel, or stand in a line opposite one another. Each child grasps a portion of the rope as in traditional tug-of-war. The children then pull with even pressure and move forward and backward while singing *Row, row, row your boat*. The object is to maintain an even pressure on the rope as it is moved and not knock down the opponent.

Song
Row, row, row your boat
Gently down the stream
Merrily, merrily, merrily, merrily
Life is but a dream.

Teacher Observations

Body Awareness: Does the child perceive how hard to pull on the rope to keep it taut?

Perception of Movement: Is the child able to stabilize shoulders and hips to maintain an upright position?

Beginning Jump Rope Games

Equipment

Jump rope, 12–15 feet long—one for each group of eight to ten children

Activity

Inside Outside

Two children turn the rope in a consistent rhythmical manner. The remaining children form a line and run through the rope without letting the rope touch them.

Cue the children to begin running when they hear the rope touch the ground. It may be helpful to mark start and stop lines.

Teacher Observations

Motor Planning: Is the child able to time when to run through the rope without being touched by the rope?

Perception of Movement: Is the child able to make the necessary anticipatory body movements before running through the rope?

Beginning Jump Rope Games

Equipment

Jump the shot—one for each group of six to eight children (see Appendix A)

Activity

Jump the Shot

Floor markers for each child are arranged in a circle. The teacher or a child squats in the center of the circle and spins the rope so that each child jumps the shot as it passes by.

Teacher Observations

Motor Planning: Can the child time the movements in order to jump sequentially?

Ocular Control: Can the child watch the shot as it approaches?

Perception of Movement: Can the child maintain balance when jumping?

Beginning Jump Rope Games

Equipment

Jump rope, 6 feet long—one for each child

Activity

Lasso Jump

The children shorten their ropes by holding both ends together. They then hold the ropes at their sides with the looped end touching the ground. The rope is twirled, using wrist action. As the rope hits the ground, the child jumps. This activity promotes good timing and rhythm for more advanced jump rope games.

Clue the children to bend their knees and jump each time they hear the rope hit the ground.

Teacher Observations

Auditory Processing: Is the child able to attend to the slapping sound of the rope?

Motor Planning: Is the child able to initiate and maintain the twirling motion with the rope?

Jump Rope Games

Equipment

Jump rope, 12–15 feet long—one for each group of four to six children
Masking tape marker

Activity

Blue Bells

To the tune of *Bluebells, cockle shells,* two rope turners swing the rope back and forth but not overhead. Allow the children to practice jumping in rhythm to the song and the swinging rope before expecting them to jump with a full turn of the rope. When accuracy is established, turn the rope a full turn as the word "over" is sung.

Easy Overhead

One child and one adult turn the rope in a full circle. The child jumping stands on the masking tape marker placed on the floor at the middle of the rope. The child jumping is asked to stay on the marker.

To assist in proper timing, give the verbal cue "and jump." Say the word "and" as the rope approaches the overhead arch and "jump" as the rope is on the downward swing. Encourage the child to watch the arm of the adult who is turning the rope. When the arm is on the downward swing, the child jumps. To ensure success, allow the child to pause after each jump, if necessary.

Teacher Observations

Motor Planning: Is the child able to time the jumps to the auditory and visual cues of the turning rope?

Perception of Movement: Can the child maintain balance when jumping consecutively?

Jump Rope Games

Equipment

Eskimo jump rope—one for each group of six to eight children (see Appendix A)

Activity

Eskimo Jump Rope

Appoint people to be rope turners. The activity is played using a back-and-forth movement of the rope. Each child takes a turn trying to repetitively jump over the bundle attached to the center of the rope. When the children become familiar with the activity, they can jump with the rope turned in a full circle.

Teacher Observations

Motor Planning: Is the child able to time the jump to clear the bundle?

Visual-Spatial Perception: Is the child able to align the body so that he or she is in the center of the arc as the rope is swung?

Jump Rope Games

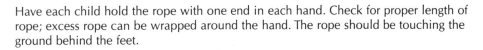

Equipment

One jump rope for each child (the length of the jump rope should reach from armpit to floor to armpit)

Activity

Individual Jump Rope

Have each child hold the rope with one end in each hand. Check for proper length of rope; excess rope can be wrapped around the hand. The rope should be touching the ground behind the feet.

The children swing the rope overhead, holding their arms out from their sides, approximately waist high. Watch for a tendency to bring the arms to the midline of the body after a swing. This can cause tripping and prevent the child from being ready for the next swing. Begin by having each child turn the rope once, let it hit the feet and step over it; progress to jumping over the rope without stopping. Cue the children to bend their knees and jump each time they hear the rope touch the ground. Encourage the children to take a preparatory rebound bounce while the rope is overhead. Try jumping with both feet together or alternating the weight from one foot to another.

Teacher Observations

Coordinating Body Sides: Can the child coordinate both hands to swing the rope overhead? Can the child coordinate the top and bottom half of his or her body to jump over the rope?

Motor Planning: Can the child time the jump to make consecutive jumps?

Advanced Jump Rope Games

Equipment

Jump rope, 12–15 feet long—one for each group of six to eight children

Activity

Cooperative Jump Rope

Two people turn the rope in a full circle. The children stand in a line and the first child in line runs in and begins to jump. After three consecutive jumps, the next child in line runs in and begins to jump along with the first child. After they have jumped three consecutive jumps, the next child in line joins them. After three consecutive jumps another child joins those already jumping. This continues as long as no one fails to jump rope. The activity begins again when the jumping group misses and starts with those who haven't had a turn.

Teacher Observations

Motor Planning: Is the child able to jump on the balls of the feet in a bouncing rhythmic pattern?

Visual-Spatial Perception: Is the child able to maintain proper spacing while jumping with another child?

Advanced Jump Rope Games

Equipment

Jump rope, 12–15 feet long—two for each group of ten to twelve children

Activity

Egg Beater

Four rope turners are designated. The ropes are held at right angles to one another and turned simultaneously so that they hit the ground together. The child jumping enters from the corner where the ropes are turning toward him or her. After jumping in the center several times, the child exits to the opposite corner.

Teacher Observations

Motor Planning: Is the child able to correctly time when to enter the turning ropes? Are the rope turners successful in synchronizing the rope turning?

Visual-Spatial Perception: Is the child able to perceive the center of the crossed ropes?

Advanced Jump Rope Games

Equipment

Two or more jump ropes, 12–15 feet long

Activity

Multiple Jump Rope

Appoint two rope turners for each rope. The ropes are spaced 10 to 12 feet apart. They are turned in full circle, hitting the floor simultaneously. Each child takes a turn running through the moving rope.

To increase the difficulty, the child may stop to jump a designated number of times in each rope.

Teacher Observations

Motor Planning: Is the child able to continue running through the ropes without losing momentum?

Ocular Control: Can the child visually track the ropes as they turn in order to successfully time his or her entrance?

Advanced Jump Rope Games

Equipment

Jump rope, 12–15 feet long—one for each group of six to eight children

Activity

Stunt Jump

Two people turn the rope in a full circle. The child jumping is given a specific sequence of actions to perform while jumping. These may include such things as touching the ground, turning around, clapping hands, and slapping the knees or feet. Familiar jump rope rhymes may be incorporated. Other children may be asked to join the child who is jumping.

For the advanced jumpers, running in and out may be added. To meet the needs of the whole class, it may be better to have the more advanced jumpers use individual jump ropes.

Teacher Observations

Auditory Processing: Can the child follow directions to the song and stay in rhythm?

Coordinating Body Sides: Can the child coordinate arms and feet together when turning the rope?

Jump Rope Rhymes

Bluebells, Cockle Shells

Bluebells, cockle shells,
    Eevy, ivy, over.
(Rope is swung back and forth until "over," then it goes full circle.)

Bread and Butter

Bread and butter,
    Sugar and spice,
How many people
    Think I'm nice?
One, two, three . . .
    (Continue counting.)

Cinderella

Cinderella dressed in yellow
    Went downstairs to kiss her fellow.
How many kisses did she get?
    One, two, three . . .
(Continue counting.)

Cinderella dressed in lace
    Went upstairs to powder her face.
How many pounds did it take?
    One, two, three . . .

Cinderella dressed in red
    Went downstairs to bake some bread.
How many loaves did she bake?
    One, two, three . . .

Doggies

Bulldog, poodle, bow wow wow.
    How many doggies have we now?
One, two, three . . .
    (Continue counting.)

Continued on page 157

Jump Rope Rhymes

Continued from page 156

Down in the Valley

Down in the valley,
    Where the green grass grows
There sat (child's name)
    As pretty as a rose;
She sang, she sang,
    She sang so sweet,
Along came (child's name)
    And kissed her on the cheek.
How many kisses did she get?
    One, two, three . . .
(Continue counting.)

Dutch Girl

I'm a little Dutch Girl
    Dressed in blue;
And these are the things
    I like to do:
Salute to the captain,
    Bow to the queen,
And turn my back
    To the mean old king.

Engine Number Nine

Engine, engine Number Nine,
    Goin' down the Chicago Line,
See it sparkle, see it shine,
    Engine, engine Number Nine.
If the train should jump the track,
    Will I get my money back?
Yes, no, maybe so . . .
    (The word that the jumper misses on is the answer.)

Grace, Grace, Dressed in Lace

Grace, Grace, dressed in lace
    Went upstairs to powder her face.
How many boxes did she use?
    One, two, three . . .
(Continue counting.)

Continued on page 158

Jump Rope Rhymes

Continued from page 157

Hoppity, Hop

Hoppity hop to the barber shop.
   How many hops before I stop?
One, two, three . . .
   (Continue counting.)

I Came to a River

I came to a river
   I couldn't get across.
I paid ten dollars
   For an old blind horse.
I jumped on its back
   And its bones went crack.

We all played the fiddle
   Till the boat came back.
The boat came back,
   We all jumped in.

The boat turned over,
   And we all fell out.

Ice Cream Soda

Ice cream soda, Delaware punch,
   Tell me the name of your honeybunch.
A, B, C, D, E, . . .
   (The letter on which the jumper misses is the first letter
   of the honeybunch's name.)

I Love Coffee

I love coffee,
   I love tea,
I want (child's name)
   To come in with me.

Continued on page 159

158   Jump Rope Games

Jump Rope Rhymes

Continued from page 158

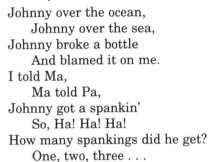

Johnny Over the Ocean

Johnny over the ocean,
    Johnny over the sea,
Johnny broke a bottle
    And blamed it on me.
I told Ma,
    Ma told Pa,
Johnny got a spankin'
    So, Ha! Ha! Ha!
How many spankings did he get?
    One, two, three . . .
(Continue counting.)

Keep the Kettle Boiling

Keep the kettle boiling,
    Be on time!
(The rope keeps turning as consecutive jumpers run in and out without losing the rhythm.)

Lady, Lady

Lady, lady at the gate,
    Eating cherries from a plate.
How many cherries did she eat?
    One, two, three . . .
(Continue counting.)

Lady Bug, Lady Bug

Lady bug, lady bug, turn around.
    Lady bug, lady bug, touch the ground.
Lady bug, lady bug, fly away home.
    Lady bug, lady bug, go upstairs.
Lady bug, lady bug, say your prayers.
    Lady bug, lady bug, turn out the light.
Lady bug, lady bug, say goodnight.

Mabel, Mabel

Mabel, Mabel, set the table
    Just as fast as you are able.
And don't forget the RED HOT PEPPERS!
    (Jump as fast as possible.)

Continued on page 160

Jump Rope Rhymes

Continued from page 159

Miss Lucy Had a Baby

Miss Lucy had a baby,
  (One child is jumping.)
His name was Tiny Tim.
  She put him in the bathtub
To see if he could swim.
  He drank up all the water.
He ate up all the soap.
  He tried to eat the bathtub,
But it wouldn't go down his throat.
  Miss Lucy called the doctor.
(Doctor runs in.)
  Miss Lucy called the nurse.
(Nurse runs in.)
  Miss Lucy called the lady with the alligator purse.
(Lady runs in.)
  "Mumps," says the doctor.
(All jump together.)
  "Measles," says the nurse.
"Nothing," says the lady with the alligator purse.
  Out runs the doctor.
(Doctor runs out.)
  Out runs the nurse.
(Nurse runs out.)
  Out runs Miss Lucy and the lady with the alligator purse.
(Lucy and lady run out.)

Mother, Mother, I Am Able

Mother, Mother, I am able
  To stand on a chair and set the table.
Daughter, daughter, don't forget
  Salt, vinegar, and red hot pepper!
(Regular jumping until "pepper.")

Polly Put the Kettle On

Polly put the kettle on
  And have a cup of tea.
In comes (child's name)
  And out goes me!

Continued on page 161

Jump Rope Rhymes

Continued from page 160

Rooms for Rent

Rooms for rent
    Inquire within.
When I move out,
    (Child's name) moves in.

Snowman

Snowman, Snowman,
    Big and round.
How many inches
    Are you around?
One, two, three . . .
    (Continue counting.)

Spanish Dancer

Not last night but the night before,
    Twenty-four robbers came knockin' at my door.
As I ran out, they ran in,
    (The jumper runs out, then in again.)
And this is what they said:
    Spanish dancer, do the splits,
Spanish dancer, do high kicks,
    Spanish dancer, touch the ground,
Spanish dancer, run out of town.
    (The jumper runs out.)

Teddy Bear

Teddy Bear, Teddy Bear,
    Turn around.
Teddy Bear, Teddy Bear,
    Touch the ground.
Teddy Bear, Teddy Bear,
    Show your shoe.
Teddy Bear, Teddy Bear,
    That will do!

Teddy Bear, Teddy Bear,
    Go upstairs.
Teddy Bear, Teddy Bear,
    Say your prayers.
Teddy Bear, Teddy Bear,
    Switch off the light.
Teddy Bear, Teddy Bear,
    Say goodnight.

Continued on page 162

Jump Rope Rhymes

Continued from page 161

Turkey, Turkey

Turkey, Turkey on the gate,
    Let (Child's name) guess your weight.
One, two, three . . .
    (Continue counting.)

Oral Motor
Activities

Oral Motor Activities

Primary Sensory and Motor Components Challenged in Each Activity

	AUDITORY PROCESSING	BODY AWARENESS	COORDINATING BODY SIDES	FINE MOTOR	MOTOR PLANNING	OCULAR CONTROL	ORAL MOTOR SKILLS	PERCEPTION OF MOVEMENT	PERCEPTION OF TOUCH	VISUAL-SPATIAL PERCEPTION
Animal Funny Faces					◆				◆	
Bubble Blowers			◆			◆	◆			
Bubble Cups						◆	◆			
Cotton Ball Relay					◆	◆	◆			
Hula Hoop Tag		◆			◆	◆				
Let's Have a Party							◆		◆	
Lipstick Licks		◆			◆		◆		◆	
Microphone Magic	◆				◆					
Peek-a-Boo		◆							◆	
Sprinkle Lips					◆				◆	
Straw Painting		◆				◆				
Tea Party				◆			◆		◆	
Tug of War					◆		◆			

Animal Funny Faces

Equipment

Mirrors

Stuffed, plastic, or cut-out animals—one for each child

Activity

The children imitate animal sounds and funny faces while looking in the mirror. The animals are used to generate interest and encourage communication. The mirrors are used to stimulate awareness of the face, jaw, lips, and tongue during speech. Try slow repetitions of the same sounds. "Moo, moo, moo," or "Meeow, meeow, meeow, meeow." Some adults have a tendency to become bored with slow repetition; the key in this activity is to slow down and provide silly repetition in imitation of one another and in front of the mirror. Try "baa," "oink," "grrr," "ruff," "hiss," "quack," "hee-haw," and "neigh."

Old MacDonald can be used to stimulate animal funny faces. Children with delayed speech will not be able to keep up with this song. It is important to try to stimulate communication at the level of the child. Therefore, in many situations, more time will be devoted to multiple repetitions of E-I-E-I-O and the animal sound. Each child works in front of a mirror and the adult makes individual contact with each child. Children have fun using their hands to accentuate the funny faces while singing E-I-E-I-O. Have the children hold air in their cheeks for a funny face and gently tap on the cheeks; this creates extra tactile and body awareness of the face and jaw.

Teacher Observations

Motor Planning: Is the child able to imitate the animal sounds or funny faces?

Perception of Touch: How does the child react to the tactile variations in the stuffed animals? Does the child avoid touching his or her face or react negatively to touch?

Bubble Blowers

Equipment

Bubble solution with a wand—one for each adult
Plastic picnic spoons—one for each child

Activity

The children sit or stand around the adult. Each child is given a turn to blow through the bubble wand. To add challenge, the children can try to catch the bubbles by clapping their hands onto the bubble. The children also can try to catch a bubble with a plastic spoon.

This activity can be modified in a number of ways. First, the adult can control the level of difficulty by adjusting the distance of the wand from the lips. The recommended range is between $\frac{1}{2}$ inch and 6 inches from the child, with the level of difficulty increasing with distance. If a child cannot blow a bubble at all, a bubble is blown for them and the child attempts to blow the bubble while it is on the wand to make it wobble or come entirely off of the wand. The bubble can be passed from student to student. The teacher can work with one bubble or many bubbles depending on how the activity is set up.

In a less controlled situation, each student can be given a small cup of bubble solution and a wand, then try to blow as many bubbles as he or she likes from a distance of his or her choice. A child-controlled wand may be important for individual practice but should not be substituted for the quality of practice that a teacher, parent, or therapist can provide.

Teacher Observations

Coordinating Body Sides: Can the child coordinate the clapping of two hands to capture a bubble?

Ocular Control: Is the child able to keep his or her eyes on the bubble targeted, or does he or she randomly swat at bubbles?

Oral Motor Skills: Is the child able to blow enough air to move or form the bubble? Does the child attempt to suck in instead of blow out?

Bubble Cups

Equipment

Plastic straws—one for each child
Clear plastic cups—one for each child
Water, juice, or milk
Paper towels and washcloths

Activity

Pour a small amount of liquid into a cup, approximately ¼ to ½ full. Give each child a straw and tell him or her to blow bubbles until the cup is filled; a clear plastic cup with a lid will reduce spilling. The goal of this activity is to have the child expel enough air to create bubbles while sealing the lips on the straw. Encourage the child to hold the straw with the lips and not the teeth.

After this activity, have each child touch, tap, wipe, and scrub his or her face with a damp paper towel or washcloth. This stimulates body awareness of the face, jaw, and lips, and teaches independence in self-care.

Teacher Observations

Ocular Control: Does the child watch the bubbles as they are being formed?

Oral Motor Skills: Can the child purse the lips around the straw to maintain a lip seal? Can the child sustain enough air force to blow bubbles?

Cotton Ball Relay

Equipment

Small cotton balls—one for each child
Straws—one for each child
Masking tape or chalk

Activity

Using masking tape or chalk, make two lines to designate a start point and a finish point. This can be done on the floor, carpet, or a table top. Place a cotton ball behind the start line. Each child is positioned behind the cotton ball and, using a straw, blows the cotton ball forward to the finish line.

Cotton Ball Soccer

Students can choose a partner and try to blow the cotton ball back and forth, trying to "score" on one another by blowing the cotton ball off the table or over the line on the opposite side.

For variation, try feathers, foam packing pieces, table tennis balls, Wiffle® golf balls, foam balls, or paper balls. Straws come in various diameters, allowing one to add or subtract resistance. Different body positions may make it easier or more difficult to blow. Observe for differences in sitting supported at a table as opposed to lying prone on the floor. Some students may need extra support and stabilization in order to practice blowing.

Teacher Observations

Motor Planning: Can the child plan a course to the finish line with the cotton ball? Can the child exhale instead of inhale when propelling the cotton ball?

Ocular Control: Is the child able to visually direct the straw to aim at the cotton ball?

Oral Motor Skills: Can the child purse the lips and use enough air to move the cotton ball?

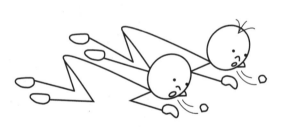

Hula Hoop Tag

Equipment

Hula hoops—one for each group
Straws—one for each child
Table tennis balls, cotton balls, or wads of paper—one for each child

Activity

For each group of children, place one hula hoop on the floor. The children gather around the hula hoop, lying prone on their stomachs or kneeling on hands and knees. Each child has a straw and begins to blow his or her table tennis ball to tag another ball. Students can blow with or without a straw. It may be difficult for some children to blow while lying in a prone position. If this is the case, substitute a smaller plastic ring for the hula hoop and have the children sit with good postural support at a table.

This exercise strengthens lip rounding and helps to exercise the tongue. When one blows out, the tongue automatically retracts, and this is an important tongue motion for beginning speech. Watch for children attempting to hold the straw with the teeth instead of the lips.

Teacher Observations

Body Awareness: Is the child able to maintain lip closure on the straw in order to blow air? Is the child able to blow out instead of suck in?

Motor Planning: Does the child aim purposefully and with an obvious plan to try to hit another ball or is he or she blowing randomly?

Ocular Control: Can the child maintain visual attention on the table tennis ball and coordinate his or her eyes and hands to propel the ball?

Let's Have a Party

Equipment

Crushed ice snow cones
Party blowers
Pinwheels
Frozen juice bars
Noisemakers
Toothettes (small sponges on a stick)
Toothbrushes
Whistles
Individual storage containers

Activity

Pretend to have a party. Decorate the area with a few balloons. Some children may be able to help blow up the balloons. Have a party favor bag or plastic cup container ready for each child. To control the fun and avoid chaos, give each child one party favor at a time. Do not allow children to share or exchange party favors after they are used. Practice blowing the party blowers until they fully extend. Noise makers can be played with randomly or in a specific pattern, for example, Blow, Blow, Shhh; Blow, Blow, Shhh. Try making noises to nursery rhyme tunes.

Serve crushed ice snow cones or frozen juice bars. The cold feeling will help to stimulate the muscles around the mouth. Continue practicing with the party favors. Toothettes are small sponges on a stick used to massage gums and clean baby teeth. Have the students massage their gums and teeth with a toothette or a soft toothbrush. Have party napkins ready so that the children can wipe their faces when necessary.

Store the party favors in separate bags, individually marked. Be sure to rinse and dry the favors thoroughly before closing the bag because germs breed in moist, closed areas. A better alternative is to use separate containers such as large paper cups or milk cartons for storage.

Teacher Observations

Oral Motor Skills: Is the child able to coordinate the lips and air flow from the diaphragm to make a noise? Can the child make a noise in a pattern? Is the child able to extend the party blower?

Perception of Touch: Does the child react in a defensive manner to the ice, toothette, or toothbrush? Will the child willingly and effectively use the napkin?

Lipstick Licks

Equipment

Cotton swab—one for each child
Lip balm or petroleum jelly
Peanut butter, jelly, honey
One mirror for each child

Activity

Give each child a cotton swab with a small amount of lip balm on it. Have the students put the lip balm on their upper and lower lips while looking in the mirror. Next, have the children imitate kissing, smacking, and simple sounds. Try ma-ma, ba-ba, baby, bee-bee, boo-boo, and pa-pa. Students also can lick their lips in an up-and-down or circular motion.

Teacher Observations

Body Awareness: Can the child get the lip balm onto the lips adequately?

Motor Planning: Is the child able to imitate the sounds and the lip movements?

Oral Motor Skills: Is the child able to make the tongue touch the top and bottom lip? Can the tongue move in a circular motion around the lips?

Perception of Touch: Does the child complain of having to touch the lips with the cotton swab and lip balm?

Microphone Magic

Equipment

Microphones, made of decorated paper towel rolls
Microphone connected to a tape recorder (optional)

Activity

The children are encouraged to use the microphone while singing songs. The teacher can approach each child and hold up the microphone to the child's mouth and wait for the child to respond. Sometimes a nonverbal child will attempt to make sounds when given a stimulus such as a microphone. Favorite songs include *Barbara Ann* (Beach Boys, 1986), *La Bamba* (Valens, R., 1959), and *Witch Doctor* (Chipmunks, 1993). Try singing two-syllable words to the tune of *Twinkle, Twinkle, Little Star;* for example, "ma-ma, ma-ma, ma-ma-ma." For variation, practice lip poppers, "pa-pa-pa," tongue tappers, "ta-ta-ta," or back of the mouth sounds, "ka-ka-ka." Any song can be used that repeats the same sound.

Teacher Observations

Auditory Processing: Is the child aware of his or her voice being projected through the tube or microphone?

Motor Planning: Can the child produce a repetitious sound? Repetition helps establish the motor planning efforts and automatic control.

Peek-a-Boo

Equipment

Paper towel, dish towel, or thin fabric—one for each child
Mirrors—one for each child

Activity

The children sit in a small group. The adult begins by putting a towel over his or her own face so that the children can see what is going to happen. The adult takes the towel off and says, "Peek-a-boo!" Next, the towel is placed over the child's face, removed, and the adult says, "Peek-a-boo!" When the children are comfortable with this game, they are encouraged to find facial features while their faces are covered with the towel; for example, "Find your nose. . . . There it is!" Provide the children with good opportunities for developing sensory awareness of facial and speech muscles by tapping, touching, and gently pinching their cheeks. Mirrors are used for additional sensory awareness of the face.

For variation, try playing peek-a-boo with stuffed or plastic animals and take turns covering the animal's and child's faces. Animal sounds can be repeated and practiced.

Teacher Observations

Body Awareness: Is the child able to locate the nose, cheeks, ears, lips, and eyes without looking?

Perception of Touch: Can the child tolerate having the towel draped over the face? Does the child overreact when the face is touched?

Sprinkle Lips

Equipment

Cake decorating sprinkles
Paper plates—one for each child

Activity

Give each child a paper plate with some sprinkles on it, then have the children lick their lips and dip them into the sprinkles. If a child is able, have him or her make a few sounds with the sprinkles on the lips; the sprinkles increase awareness of the lips by adding weight and texture. To clean the lips, have the children lick their lips in a circular motion or back and forth like a windshield wiper; have the children use their tongue to clean specific places.

Teacher Observations

Motor Planning: Is the child able to plan the lip movements with the sprinkles on the lips? Is the child able to plan the tongue movements necessary to lick the lips clean?

Perception of Touch: Can the child tolerate the sprinkles on the lips? If defensive responses are noted, do not insist that the child continue; additional opportunities can be provided in the future. It is important that the children voluntarily and actively participate.

Straw Painting

Equipment

Straws—one for each child
Water colors—one box for each adult
Eye dropper or paint brush—one for each adult
Water—one cup for each adult
Construction paper—one piece for each child

Activity

Give each child a piece of white construction paper and a straw. Wet the water colors and deposit a drop of water color on each child's paper. The child then uses the straw to blow the drop of paint and create a design. More drops of paint can be added when the child is ready. The children clean their straws after each color by blowing into a cup of water.

Straws come in a variety of sizes and diameters. A straw with a smaller hole, such as a coffee stirrer, will require more oral motor and respiratory effort than a soda straw. Aquarium tubing can be cut in different lengths to present different challenge levels.

Teacher Observations

Body Awareness: Is the child able to adequately purse the lips to make a seal around the straw? Is the child able to control the air to make a design? Check to see that the straw is being held by the lips and not the teeth.

Ocular Control: Does the child look at the drop of paint and attempt to visually guide the paint while blowing through the straw?

Tea Party

Equipment

Plastic tea party set
Small plates
Pretty napkins
Bibs, if needed
Spoons and forks
Variety of finger foods—bananas, strawberries, melon, mango, papaya, vanilla cookies, angel food cake, rice cakes, crackers (animal, fish, soda), pudding, yogurt, gelatin, tea sandwiches
Beverage—juice, herb tea, milk

Activity

Set a pretty table, with a place setting for each child. Have the children put napkins in their laps. Pour each child a cup of beverage, and serve one or two finger foods at a time. Have a designated child serve the treats, one for each child. Be sure to include a variety of tastes and textures. Encourage the children to try new foods and to use forks and spoons.

Teacher Observations

Fine Motor: Can the child coordinate the use of the fork and spoon? Observe the child's grasp and ability to bring food to the mouth without spilling.

Oral Motor Skills: Can the child use the tongue to clean the food off the teeth? Is the child able to effectively chew by moving the food around in the mouth in a circular motion?

Perception of Touch: Will the child eat a variety of foods and try new foods and textures?

Tug of War

Equipment

Licorice pieces
Dental floss
Buttons

Activity

The children can work in pairs, or two children can work while the rest of the class watches. This activity works well with one pair of children for each adult. Each child puts one end of the licorice in his or her mouth, with lips closed around the licorice. The children gently try to pull the licorice out of each other's mouths. Encourage the children to hold the licorice with the lips and not the teeth.

Teacher Observations

Motor Planning: Can the child plan the movements necessary to pull gently with the head and lips?

Oral Motor Skills: Is the child able to use the lips to hold the licorice while working against resistance?

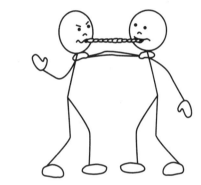

Tool Activities

Tool Activities

Primary Sensory and Motor Components Challenged in Each Activity

	AUDITORY PROCESSING	BODY AWARENESS	COORDINATING BODY SIDES	FINE MOTOR	MOTOR PLANNING	OCULAR CONTROL	ORAL MOTOR SKILLS	PERCEPTION OF MOVEMENT	PERCEPTION OF TOUCH	VISUAL-SPATIAL PERCEPTION
Clothespin Games				◆		◆				
Cooking		◆	◆		◆					
Finger Painting			◆						◆	
Folding Art			◆							◆
Modeling Clay Activities				◆					◆	
Paper Strips			◆	◆	◆					◆
Pop Beads				◆						◆
Rub Art		◆		◆						
Sewing Projects		◆	◆		◆					
Shape Art					◆					◆
Spray Bottle Games				◆		◆				
Stamp Art		◆		◆						◆
Sticker Art				◆						◆
Stringing				◆					◆	
Tweezers, Tongs, and Chopsticks				◆					◆	
Weaving			◆	◆						◆
Wishing Well				◆						◆

Clothespin Games

Equipment

Clothespin—one for each child
Cardboard shape or picture—one or more for each class

Activity

The children sit in a circle, close enough to pass an object from one to another. Each child is given a clothespin. The cardboard shape or picture begins around the circle by the leader attaching a clothespin to the object. Then the child sitting next to the leader attaches his or her clothespin to the object. The leader, who is holding the object with a clothespin, releases it when the child receiving the object has his or her clothespin attached. The object of the game is to pass the picture around the circle without dropping it. This can be done to music, a story, a team relay, or in a hot potato fashion.

Teacher Observations

Fine Motor: Is the child able to pinch the clothespin with enough force to open and close it?

Ocular Control: Does the child maintain visual contact throughout the passing process?

Cooking

Equipment

Appropriate cooking utensils
Specific ingredients

Activity

Choose a simple recipe that uses a variety of cooking utensils, such as plastic knives, an apple slicer, egg separator or slicer, juicer, melon baller, pancake turner, pastry tube, rolling pin, and wire whisk.

For easy set up and clean up, and for better classroom hygiene, arrange individual place settings with all necessary ingredients on a large paper plate for each child.

When possible, separate the children into small groups of two to four, with an adult to assist. Demonstrate each step of the recipe, and allow each group to complete that step before beginning the next step.

Try the no-bake recipes displayed on the following pages.

Teacher Observations

Body Awareness: Does the child use the correct amount of force necessary to roll cookie batter into balls? Is the child able to exert sufficient strength to control a pastry tube?

Coordinating Body Sides: Is the child able to use one hand to stabilize the cooking utensil while activating it with the other hand?

Motor Planning: Is the child able to effectively use the cooking utensil?

No-Bake Recipes

Ants on a Log

Equipment

Vegetable brush
Plastic knives—one for each child
Paper plates—one for each child

Ingredients

Celery
Peanut butter
Raisins

Clean the celery with a vegetable brush. Using a plastic knife, fill each celery stalk with peanut butter. Place the raisins in a row on top of the peanut butter–filled celery stalks.

Banana Bonbons

Equipment

Nut grinder or chopper
Plastic knives—one for each child
Soup bowls—one for each child
Plastic forks—one for each child
Paper plates—one for each child

Ingredients

Coating such as ground unsalted peanuts, cake decorating sprinkles, coconut, or crushed cereal
1 small jar peanut butter
4–6 firm bananas
16 ounces flavored yogurt

Banana–Peanut Butter Bonbons

Place a small amount of coating on each plate. Slice the bananas into 1-inch slices. Spread the banana slice with peanut butter until it is covered. Roll the peanut butter–covered banana slices in the coating. Place on the platter.

Banana–Coconut Bonbons

Place the coconut into a bowl. Stir the yogurt, spear a banana slice, and dip the slice into the yogurt to coat completely. Roll the banana slice in the coconut and then place it on the platter.

Continued on page 184

No-Bake Recipes

Continued from page 183

Moon Balls

Equipment

> Reclosable plastic bags—one for each student
> Rolling pins—one for each student; made of 1-inch diameter dowels six inches long
> Paper bowls
> Plastic spoons

Ingredients

> Honey
> Peanut Butter
> Powdered Milk
> Corn Flakes
> Bran Flakes

Place the corn or bran flakes in the reclosable plastic bag and crush them with a rolling pin or by squeezing the bag by hand. Give each student a paper bowl with 1 tablespoon peanut butter, 1 teaspoon honey, and 1 teaspoon powdered milk. Have the children pour the crushed corn or bran flakes into the bowl and mix the ingredients thoroughly with their hands. Form this mixture into 1-inch balls and roll the balls in the crushed corn or bran flakes.

Rice Cake Happy Faces

Equipment

> Plastic knives for each child
> Paper plates

Ingredients

> Rice cakes
> Cream cheese
> Raisins

Spread cream cheese onto the rice cakes using a plastic knife. Arrange raisins to form a happy face.

Finger Painting

Equipment

Finger paint paper
Finger paint media—liquid starch tempera paint, shaving cream, or instant pudding
Aprons or shirts

Activity

Have the children wear aprons or shirts to protect their clothes. Pour finger paint directly onto the table or onto finger paint paper.

- ◆ The children can use both hands simultaneously to paint circles or simple patterns.
- ◆ Patterns can be made by tapping individual fingers.
- ◆ Children can trace around their hands with the opposite index finger.
- ◆ Grains such as rice, cornmeal, oatmeal, and lentils can be added to provide a variety of textures.
- ◆ Prints can be made by laying newsprint or construction paper cut into shapes over the child's painting and gently rubbing the paper.

Teacher Observations

Coordinating Body Sides: Is the child able to use both hands to make simultaneous, mirrored movements?

Perception of Touch: Does the child avoid placing his or her hands into the paint? Does the child frequently ask to wash his or her hands?

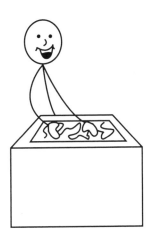

Folding Art

Equipment

Construction, typing, or wrapping paper

Activity

Give the children pre-cut and pre-marked paper to fold. Until a child can fold with precision, stay with simple fan-folded projects, such as inchworms, pop-outs, and accordion-legged animals and clowns. Emphasize the necessity of carefully folding on the line and following the directions step by step. Dotted and solid lines may be used to designate inside and outside folds.

Teacher Observations

Coordinating Body Sides: Is the child able to coordinate both hands when folding the paper?

Visual-Spatial Perception: Is the child able to correctly orient the paper?

Modeling Clay Activities

Equipment

Modeling clay
Plastic drop cloth
Plastic tubes (hair curlers)
Plastic knives
Scissors
Rolling pins
Cookie cutters
Garlic press
Egg slicers
Cookie guns

Activity

Place a plastic drop cloth on the floor under the tables. Have the children sit, kneel, or stand at the table. Give each child some of the modeling clay and allow the child to choose one or two utensils from the equipment list.

◆ Make balls or eggs by rolling a piece of clay between the palms of the hands.
◆ Make snakes by rolling a ball of clay back and forth with the palms of the hands or by pressing the clay through a plastic tube. Cut the clay snakes into discs with a plastic knife or scissors.
◆ Roll the clay with a rolling pin. Cut flat dough with cookie cutters.
◆ Press the clay through the garlic press.
◆ Press the clay into molds to make shapes.
◆ Use a cookie gun or press to make individual shapes or snakes.
◆ Cut the clay into slices with an egg slicer.

Teacher Observations

Fine Motor: Does the child have difficulty using the equipment?

Perception of Touch: Does the child avoid putting his or her hands into the clay mixture?

Continued on page 188

Modeling Clay Activities

Continued from page 187

Modeling Clay Recipe

1 cup of flour
1 teaspoon cream of tartar
$\frac{1}{2}$ cup salt
1 tablespoon oil
1 cup water
Food coloring
Scent (optional)

Mix all of the ingredients together. Heat over a very low heat, stirring constantly until the mixture begins to ball. Continue to cook the clay until it reaches the desired stiffness. Turn the clay out onto a floured surface and knead until it has cooled. Store in an airtight container.

188   Tool Activities

Paper Strips

Equipment

Scissors—one pair for each child
Paper, construction weight with pre-drawn lines

Activity

Draw a straight line on a piece of paper that is 6–8 inches long. Begin with lines that are at least $\frac{1}{8}"$–$\frac{1}{4}"$ wide, and make them as wide as necessary for the child to cut within the line. The goal of this activity is to make the child aware of the boundaries and to develop scissor skills. Strips of cut paper can be glued together to form a ring and connected to make paper chains or used for paper weaving.

Once a child has mastered cutting a straight line, reduce the width of the line until he or she can successfully cut a thin line. After mastering the cutting of straight lines, use the same approach for wide curved lines, narrow curved lines, angular lines, and circles.

Teacher Observations

Coordinating Body Sides: Is the child able to hold the paper with one hand and move the scissors forward when cutting?

Fine Motor: Does the child position the scissors on the thumb and long finger? Does the child use the index finger to stabilize the scissors?

Motor Planning: Can the child plan changes in direction?

Visual-Spatial Perception: Can the child stay on the lines?

Pop Beads

Equipment

Pop beads—six for each child
Beanbags
Bucket of water
Slotted spoon
Trigger-type spray bottle

Activity

◆ The children can try to duplicate pop bead designs according to color, shape, and sequence.
◆ Pop beads can be used to measure objects in the room and compare various sizes and lengths.
◆ Have the children connect the pop beads to make various-sized rings. Place the rings on the floor and use them for targets. Have the children toss beanbags into the pop bead rings.
◆ Individual pop beads can be used to toss into targets, such as baskets, buckets, and rings.
◆ Float individual pop beads in a bucket of water. Have the children take turns fishing for pop beads with a slotted spoon.
◆ Float individual pop beads in a bucket of water. Have the children take turns trying to propel a pop bead in the water by squirting at it with a spray bottle.

Teacher Observations

Fine Motor: Does the child have the strength and coordination to propel the pop bead with the spray bottle?

Visual-Spatial Perception: Is the child able to accurately use the pop beads to measure objects and compare sizes? Is the child able to judge the distance to the target when tossing the beanbags or pop beads?

Rub Art

Equipment

Crayons, pencils, chalk
Relief designs—leaves, rubber bands, string, paper shapes, paper clips, confetti
Dried-glue relief drawings
Paper

Activity

The child places paper over a design to be transferred and rubs the flat side of the crayon over the paper until the design's impression is visible.

For variation, integrate this activity into a lesson on numbers, letters, spelling words, or math problems. Write the particular item on heavy cardboard with hot glue from a glue gun or with white school glue. When it is dry, have the child make a rubbing. The cardboard can be cut into smaller pieces with numbers and math signs added to form equations.

Teacher Observations

Body Awareness: Is the child able to judge the amount of pressure needed to make the impression visible?

Fine Motor: Is the child able to securely hold the side of the crayon when rubbing the crayon across the paper?

Sewing Projects

Equipment

Yarn, shoelaces, string, thread
Needles, bobby pins
Paper, felt
Hole punch

Activity

Cut the string into 12- to 18-inch pieces. Tape one end of the yarn, and thread the taped end through a bobby pin or large-eyed needle; then double the yarn and tie the ends into a knot.

Paper Packets

Staple together two pieces of construction paper, and mark three edges of the paper with spots to be punched for holes. Have the children punch holes on the spots and sew together the three sides of the paper packet; remove the staples.

Felt and Button Projects

Buttons can be sewn onto felt to make projects such as headbands and bracelets. The child sews the buttons on a strip of felt and secures them with a knot on the reverse side. Attach the ends of the felt together by sewing a button on one end and cutting a small hole on the other end.

Teacher Observations

Body Awareness: Can the child exert enough pressure to use the hole punch? Is the child able to automatically feel where to insert the thread from the bottom coming up?

Coordinating Body Sides: Can the child stabilize the project with one hand and sew with the other hand?

Motor Planning: Does the child have difficulty sewing through the holes in the proper organized, planned sequence?

Shape Art

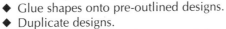

Equipment

Construction paper
Tissue paper
Wallpaper
Wrapping paper
Glue

Activity

Give each child a piece of paper, some glue, and a variety of geometric shapes. Choose an activity from the following list according to the child's ability.

- ◆ Glue shapes onto paper, creating random designs.
- ◆ Glue shapes onto pre-outlined designs.
- ◆ Duplicate designs.
- ◆ Experiment with the placement of shapes to create identifiable objects.
- ◆ Have the children describe what they are going to create. Provide several examples when giving directions, but do not allow the children to directly copy the teacher.

Teacher Observations

Motor Planning: Can the child plan a design and follow through with the plan?

Visual-Spatial Perception: Can the child duplicate designs? Can the child create identifiable objects?

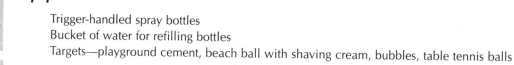
Spray Bottle Games

Equipment

Trigger-handled spray bottles
Bucket of water for refilling bottles
Targets—playground cement, beach ball with shaving cream, bubbles, table tennis balls

Activity

◆ Line up the children in groups of two or three, and give each group one spray bottle. The children use the spray bottle to draw letters and numbers on the cement.
◆ Place a beach ball on top of the bucket, 4 to 6 feet from the children. Draw a happy face, number, or letter on the ball with shaving cream, and have the children take turns squirting the water at the beach ball until the cream is washed off.
◆ Have the children spray a stream of water to pop bubbles blown by the teacher.
◆ The children can have relay races by propelling a table tennis ball with a stream of water over a designated finish line.

Teacher Observations

Fine Motor: Is the child able to repeatedly squeeze the spray bottle trigger?

Ocular Control: Does the child maintain visual contact with the object that is being sprayed?

Stamp Art

Equipment

Stamps—fingers, hands, toes, feet; halved potatoes, apples, oranges, lemons; sponges; blocks of wood or dowels with rubber designs on the bottoms; pencils with unused eraser tips

Paper—newsprint, butcher paper, computer paper, quadrille paper

Ink—water-based ink pads, tempera paint, acrylic paint

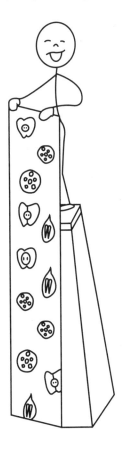

Activity

Have the children use stamps to repeat random designs on large pieces of paper, duplicate specific designs, or copy precise designs on quadrille paper.

Teacher Observations

Body Awareness: Does the child push too hard or too softly with the stamp?

Fine Motor: Is the child able to maintain a consistent grasp on the stamp to make a complete impression?

Visual-Spatial Perception: Can the child space the stamp designs accurately when precision is required?

Sticker Art

Equipment

Stickers
Sticker design samples
Wax paper

Activity

- ◆ The children may choose a design and then outline the design with sticker dots.
- ◆ The children can place stickers on a picture to match appropriate shapes.
- ◆ The teacher duplicates simple designs on graph paper. The children are then asked to position the stickers accurately within the lines.

Note: Wax paper can be placed over sticker projects so that designs can be used again.

Teacher Observations

Fine Motor: Does the child have adequate fine grasp to pick up stickers, using both the thumb and index finger?

Visual-Spatial Perception: Can the child place stickers in the correct position on the paper?

Stringing

Equipment

String, thread, yarn—24 inches long
Needles or tape
Scissors
Toothpicks
Stringable objects—cereal, modeling clay beads, beads, cranberries, marshmallows, colored straws, macaroni, paper shapes, sequins, buttons

Activity

To prepare the string, the teacher either threads a needle or tapes one end of the yarn or string to form a firm point. The teacher should tie a knot in the other end of the string. The children can use the string for the following activities:

Colored Straw Necklace: Have the children cut colored straws into pieces about $\frac{1}{2}$ to 1 inch long, then string the pieces to form a necklace.

Paper Shape Necklace: The teacher should mark a spot on each paper shape, then have the children punch a hole on the spot; hole reinforcers can be used to prevent the holes from tearing. Try interspersing paper shapes with other stringable objects such as cut straws.

Confetti Necklace: Have the children use a needle and thread to string confetti made from the hole punch.

Modeling Clay: Have the children roll out clay snakes, then cut the snakes into $\frac{1}{2}$-inch pieces. Use a toothpick to poke a hole in the center of each clay piece. Let the clay dry and then have the children string the beads.

Painted Salad Macaroni: Have the children paint macaroni pieces with tempera paint. Let the pieces dry and then let the children string them.

Teacher Observations

Fine Motor: Does the child have any difficulty using tools such as needles, scissors, and a hole punch?

Perception of Touch: Does the child resist touching or using any of the materials?

Tweezers, Tongs, and Chopsticks

Equipment

Tweezers, tongs, pair of chopsticks—one for each child
Objects to pick up or carry—popped corn, beans, cereal, cotton balls, paper wads,
    small blocks
Target or canister—one for each child or small group

Activity

The object of this activity is to provide the child with many opportunities to pick up
objects with a pincer. Games to be played using the tongs include tic-tac-toe, counting,
hot potato, stacking blocks, and carrying objects. Transferring and stacking objects with
tongs challenges joint stability and visual tracking, and provides an opportunity to
practice sustained ocular pursuits. Placing objects along a line, such as within squares
on graph paper, helps to reinforce recognition of boundaries.

Teacher Observations

Fine Motor: Is the child able to use a tripod grasp with the tweezers or tongs? Can the
child accurately time the opening and closing motions?

Perception of Touch: Can the child maintain enough pressure on the tweezers or tongs
to hold an object and not look at his or her hands?

Weaving

Equipment

Construction paper—two pieces for each child
Scissors
Paste or glue

Activity

Cut one piece of the construction paper in a desired shape, for example, a heart, shamrock, or triangle. Fold the paper shape in half and mark a 1-inch margin at the open end. Make straight cuts from the fold to the margin, about 1-inch apart; this is the warp. Cut a second piece of construction paper lengthwise into ½-inch strips; this is the weft.

Weave a strip of the weft paper over, then under the warp. Weave a second strip next to the first, starting under, then over. Repeat this process, continuing to alternate the over-and-under pattern. When the entire warp is filled with strips, trim the excess and glue the ends to secure.

As the children become more adept at weaving, variations in the patterns can be made by skipping one or more spaces on the warp, changing colors, or using various materials other than paper for the weft.

Teacher Observations

Coordinating Body Sides: Is the child able to use both hands together to easily manipulate the materials?

Fine Motor: Does the child have good finger dexterity?

Visual-Spatial Perception: Is the child able to repeat the designated weaving pattern?

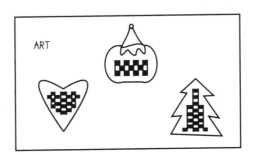

Wishing Well

Equipment

Bucket—filled with 8 inches of water
Cup
Clothespins—one for each child
Pennies—six to eight for each child

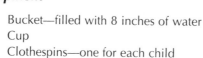

Activity

Place a cup or can in the bottom of the bucket of water and have the children gather around the bucket. Give each child a clothespin and a penny. The child must hold the penny with a clothespin and release the penny so that it falls into the cup. Once the child has taken a turn, he or she is rewarded with another penny for following directions and goes to the end of the line.

Teacher Observations

Fine Motor: Can the child pinch a clothespin between the thumb and index and middle fingers in order to release the penny?

Visual-Spatial Perception: Does the child align the clothespin over the cup?

Appendix A

Basic Classroom Equipment

Gross Motor

Most of the equipment needed to play the gross motor games in this book can be contained in a single 5-gallon bucket. Having this basic equipment on hand makes it easy to prepare for and then modify an activity.

Balloons
Balls in a variety of sizes, weights, and textures—beach, tennis, and playground balls
Beanbags
Bleach bottle scoops
Clothing with buttons, snaps, and zippers
Clothespins
Eskimo Jump Rope
Jump rope made of woven soft cotton; avoid hard plastic, acrylic, or nylon
Jump the Shot Rope
Plastic hoops 15 to 20 inches in diameter
Rhythm sticks made of half-inch dowels
Start and finish lines: masking tape, chalk
Streamers
Two-handed bat
Weighted plastic pop bottles
Yarn

Fine Motor

Building blocks
Cardboard boxes, shoe boxes, facial tissue boxes
Chalk
Chopsticks
Clothespins
Cooking utensils
Cotton balls, cotton swabs
Craft sticks
Dowels cut for rolling pins
Finger paint
Glue
Hole punch
Ink pads
Manila envelopes
Masking tape
Modeling clay

Continued on page 203

Basic Classroom Equipment

Continued from page 202

Needles
Paper: construction, lined, newsprint, quadrille, tissue paper
Paper bowls, paper plates
Pennies
Reclosable plastic bags
Scissors
Sponges
Spray bottles
Stickers
Straws
String, yarn, thread
Textures, beans, lentils, rice, popcorn
Unsharpened pencils with erasers
Writing tools: pencils, crayons, markers

Oral Motor

Animals: plastic, stuffed, or laminated pictures
Bubbles with bubble wands
Cake decorating sprinkles
Cotton balls, cotton swabs
Food to have on hand: cereals, peanut butter, honey, crackers, pudding
Licorice
Lip balm, petroleum jelly
Liquids: Water, juice, milk
Lollipops
Masking tape
Mirrors
Music and noise makers that require blowing to activate
Paper plates
Paper towels, paper towel rolls
Pinwheels
Plastic cups with lids
Plastic spoons
Party favors that require blowing to activate
Plastic gloves
Plastic tea party set
Plastic 12" diameter hoop or larger hula hoop
Straws
Table tennis balls
Toothbrushes
Whistles

Beanbags

Materials

Heavy broadcloth, canvas, denim, or corduroy
Filling—pinto beans, rice, popcorn, or washable plastic pellets if possible

Directions

1. Cut the fabric: 10″ × 5″ for small beanbags; 10″ × 20″ for large beanbags. (See Figure 1.)

2. Fold the fabric in half with the right sides together and stitch $\frac{1}{2}$-inch seams around two of the open sides. (See Figure 2.)

3. Turn the beanbag fabric right side out. Fold $\frac{1}{2}$ inch of the unstitched edge inside and press.

4. Top stitch the unstitched edge, leaving a hole large enough for a funnel. (See Figure 3.)

5. Fill small beanbags with one cup of filling; large beanbags with three cups.

6. Top stitch over the filling hole.

It is better to buy washable premade beanbags filled with plastic pellets.

Figure 1

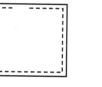

Figure 2

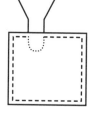

Figure 3

Bleach Bottle Scoop

Materials

One clean bleach bottle
Nine-inch dowel or piece of wood to fit through the handle of the bleach bottle
Cloth tape

Directions

1. Cut the bottom of the bottle out on a diagonal.

2. Insert the dowel or board into the handle.

3. Secure the handle with cloth tape.

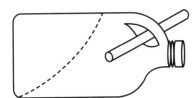

Eskimo Jump Rope

Materials

One jump rope, 12–15 feet long
One pillowcase
Plastic or cloth tape
Newspaper

Directions

1. Make a 2″ slit in the center of the sewn end of the pillowcase.

2. Center the pillowcase on the length of the rope.

3. Bunch the sewn end of the pillowcase tightly around the rope and secure with tape. (Tape the pillowcase fabric 2–3 inches from the edge.)

4. Fill the pillowcase with crumpled newspaper.

5. Bunch the open end of the pillowcase, and secure it with tape.

6. Tie a loop at each end of the rope to form handles.

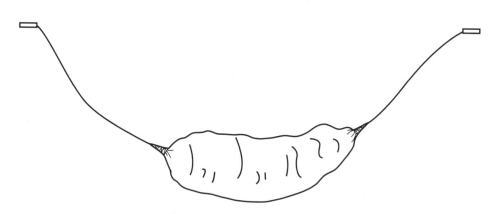

Jump the Shot Rope

Materials

One-half pound beanbag
One 6' jump rope
Thread and needle

Directions

1. Make a 2″ slit in one edge of the beanbag's stitched seams.

2. Tie a double knot in one end of the jump rope.

3. Poke the knot through the slit in the beanbag.

4. Triple stitch the beanbag to resecure the opened seam.

5. Tie a looped handle on the end of the jump rope.

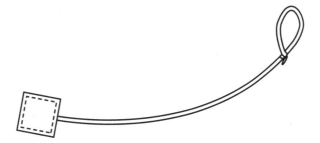

Rhythm Sticks

Materials

Wooden dowels—36-inch lengths (recommended sizes: $\frac{1}{2}$″ or $\frac{5}{8}$″ diameter)
Permanent marking pens

Directions

1. Cut each dowel into three 12-inch lengths; sand the cut edges.

2. If sticks of different diameters are used in one class, color the tips of each pair of rhythm sticks with permanent marking pens for ease in sorting and for variation in game playing.

Rolling Pins

Materials

Wooden dowels—36" length; 1" diameter

Directions

1. Cut into 6" lengths, sand edges

Streamers

Materials

One 2″ × 50″ strip of crepe paper or spinnaker cloth for each streamer
One craft stick for each streamer
Newspaper
Cloth tape

Directions

1. Fold one end of the crepe paper or spinnaker cloth strip in half and attach the folded end to a craft stick with the cloth tape.

2. Wrap the craft stick in newspaper strips to build up the handle to approximately 4 inches long and $\frac{1}{2}$ inch in diameter.

3. Wrap the cloth tape around the entire newspaper "handle."

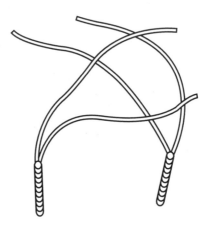

Two-Handed Bat

Materials

Two 2-liter plastic soda pop bottles
Crumpled newspaper
Cloth tape

Directions

1. Cut three inches off of the bottom of each bottle. (See Figure 1.)

2. Cut two-inch deep notches around the bottom of one of the bottles. (See Figure 2.)

3. Fill both bottles with crumpled newspaper.

4. Making sure the bottle handles are aligned, insert the bottom of the bottle with the notched edge into the bottom of the other bottle.

5. Wrap tape around the seam where the bottles join. (See Figure 3.)

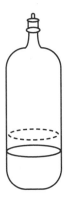

Figure 3

Figure 2

Figure 1

Weighted Plastic Pop Bottle

Materials

One 1-liter plastic soda pop bottle
One-half pound pinto beans
Cloth tape

Directions

1. Pour the pinto beans into the bottle.

2. Replace the bottle cap and seal it with cloth tape.

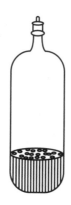
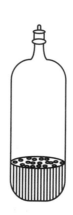

Weighted Snake

Materials

One 10″ × 38″ piece of heavy cotton fabric
3 to 5 pounds of pinto beans

Directions

1. Fold the fabric in half lengthwise and stitch along the raw edge, leaving an opening large enough to turn the fabric right side out.

2. Turn the fabric right side out and stitch around the edges to make a $\frac{1}{4}$-inch reinforced border.

3. Fill the tube loosely with the pinto beans, and stitch the opening closed.

4. Distribute the beans within the tube into three sections, and stitch vertical lines as shown on the illustration, so that the beans will not all go to one end.

5. Draw or applique a face on one end of the snake.

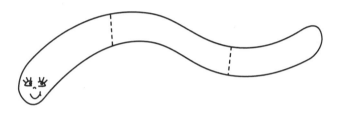

Wiffle® Ball Catcher

Materials

One 2-liter plastic soda pop bottle
One 2¾" Wiffle® ball
One 30-inch piece of kite string

Directions

1. Cut off the bottom of the bottle, leaving a 7-inch deep "catcher" bowl. (See Figure 1.)

2. Attach one end of the string to the Wiffle® ball. (See Figure 2.)

3. Attach the other end of the string to the neck of the bottle. (See Figure 2.)

Figure 1   Figure 2

Appendix B

Index of Games

Continued on page 217

Index of Games

Continued from page 216

Continued on page 218

Index of Games

Continued from page 217

Bibliography

Ayres, A. Jean. 1979. *Sensory integration and the child.* Beverly Hills, California: Western Psychological Services.

Ayers, A. Jean. 1985. *Developmental dyspraxia and adult onset apraxia.* Torrance, California: Sensory Integration International.

Ayres, A. Jean. 1989. *Sensory integration and praxis tests.* Los Angeles, California: Western Psychological Services.

Banus, Barbara S. 1979. *The developmental therapist: A prototype of the pediatric occupational therapist.* Thorofare, New Jersey: Charles B. Slack.

Benbow, Mary. 1989. *Loops and other groups.* San Antonio, Texas: Therapy Skill Builders.

Beach Boys. 1986. Barbara Ann. On *Made in U.S.A.* (record). Hollywood, California: Capitol.

Beall, Pamela C., and Susan H. Nipp. 1982. *Wee sing and play.* Los Angeles, California: Price/Stern/Sloan.

California Department of Education. 1994. *I can learn, a handbook for parents, teachers and students.* Sacramento, California: Author.

Centralia School District. 1973. *Primary physical education.* Buena Park, California: Duplicated by Orange County Department of Education.

Chipmunks. 1993. Witch Doctor. On *The Chipmunk sing alongs* (record). New York: Chipmunk records.

DeQuiros, Julio B., and Orlando L. Schrager. 1978. *Neuropsychological fundamentals in learning disabilities.* San Raphael, California: Academic Therapy Publications.

McCarney, Stephen B., Kathy Cummins Wunderlich, and Angela M. Bauer. 1994. *The teacher's resource guide.* Columbia, Missouri: Hawthorne Educational Services.

Pehoski, Charlene, and Jane Case-Smith. 1992. *Development of hand skills in the child.* Rockville, Maryland: The American Occupational Therapy Association.

Orlick, Terry. 1978. *The cooperative sports & games book.* New York: Pantheon Books.

Orlick, Terry. 1982. *The second cooperative sports & games book.* New York: Pantheon Books.

Rasmussen, Richard M., and Ronda L. Rasmussen. 1981. *The kid's encyclopedia of things to make and do.* San Diego, California: Oak Tree Publications.

Continued on page 220

Bibliography

Continued from page 219

Sherman, R. M. 1964. Step in Time. On *Walt Disney presents the original soundtrack of Mary Poppins* (record). Burbank, California: Buena Vista Records.

Valens, R. 1959. La Bamba. On *Ritchie Valens* (record). Los Angeles, California: Del-Fi.

Ventura County Special Education Service Area Consortium. September 1983. *Motor program handbook: A guide for teachers.* Ventura, California: Author.

Wirth, Marian J. 1976. *Teacher's handbook of children's games: A guide to developing perceptual-motor skills.* West Nyack, New York: Parker Publishing Co.